5N8180621061

The Art
of Wrought Metalwork
for House and Garden

1 The key of the sign-board
of the Schmirler forge

Otto Schmirler

The Art
of Wrought Metalwork
for House and Garden

Architectural Book Publishing Company
New York, 10016

Picture credits

Foto Denner: 147; Baumeister Dipl.-Ing. Durst, Wien: 712, Foto D'Paul Freuler, Basel: 636; H.P. Kumpa, Perchtoldsdorf: 37, 178, 347, 499, 500, 506, 507, 617, 628, 717, 718, 726, 727, 728, 729, 730, 731; Foto Meyer, Wien: 46, 61, 66, 114, 122, 123, 127, 144, 145, 146, 154, 172, 278, 287, 288, 390, 398, 405, 406, 418, 421, 426, 456, 486, 487, 491, 505, 571, 586, 589, 602, 604, 605, 607, 616, 625, 640; Narbutt-Lieven & Co., Wien: 109, 501; Foto-studio Otto, Wien: 30, 31, 33, 39, 40, 49, 50, 55, 56, 75, 118, 119, 139, 148, 161, 173, 174, 179, 207, 226, 242, 244, 270, 283, 394, 395, 416, 417, 420, 438, 439, 444, 445, 451, 453, 462, 463, 466, 467, 474, 484, 490, 494, 495, 496, 497, 603, 621, 622, 624, 633, 651, 660, 711. All other photographs, drawings and designs by Otto Schmirler.

First American edition 1979 by
Architectural Book Publishing Co., New York 10016

Translated by Susan C. Csoma

Library of Congress Cataloging in Publication Data

Schmirler, Otto.
    The art of wrought metalwork for house and garden.

      Translation of Schmiedekunst am Haus.
      1. Architectural ironwork. 2. Wrought-iron. I. Title.
NA3950.S3513   1979   739'.4   79-17566
ISBN 0-8038-0018-5

Published simultaneously in Canada by
Saunders of Toronto, Ltd., Don Mills, Ontario

Printed in West Germany

Inhalt

7 Vorwort

10 Geschmiedete Bildwerke

19 Gartentore

43 Briefkasten und Briefeinwurf

51 Tore und Türen

79 Laternen

115 Türgitter und
Türoberlichtgitter

135 Beschläge

149 Fenstergitter

195 Geländer und Geländerstäbe

241 Gartenmöbel

245 Brunnen, Brunnenfiguren

265 Geschmiedeter
Hausschmuck

271 Ziergitter

281 Die Burg Perchtoldsdorf

295 Vergleichende Tabelle
der Abbildungsnummern
in diesem Buch und der
Werknummern der
Kunstschmiede Schmirler

Contents

11 Preface

14 Wrought Sculptures

19 Garden Gates

43 Letter-boxes and Letter-box
Slots

51 Gates and Doors

79 Lanterns

115 Grilles for Doors and
Transom Windows

135 Iron Furnishings

149 Window Grilles

195 Balustrades and Balusters

241 Garden Furniture

245 Fountains, Wells and
Sculptural Fountain Figures

265 Wrought Decorations for the
Home

271 Ornamental Screens

281 Perchtoldsdorf Castle

295 Concordance of illustrations
and Schmirler archive
numbers

Table des matières

15 Préface

18 Œuvres d'art forgées

19 Portails de jardins

43 Boîtes aux lettres

51 Portails et portes

79 Lanternes

115 Grilles de portes et
grilles d'impostes

135 Garnitures

149 Grilles de fenêtres

195 Rampes, balustrades
et barreaux

241 Meubles de jardins

245 Puits et ornements de puits

265 Ornements en fer forgé

271 Grilles ornementales

281 Le château Perchtoldsdorf

295 Concordance des figures du
livre et de l'archive Schmirler

2

3

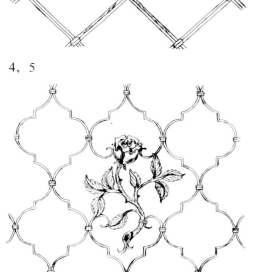

4, 5

Vorwort

Das Thema, das ich mir für dies Buch gestellt habe, ist die Eisenkunst am Bau, gestern und heute. Schmiedeeisen am Bau hat zwei Funktionen: eine schützende und eine dekorative. Beide sollen hier zur Geltung kommen. Dem schöpferischen Handwerker erwachsen daraus mannigfache Aufgaben. Denn die Architektur setzt eine ganz besondere Anpassungsfähigkeit und das Gefühl für sehr feine Abwandlungen voraus. Dies ist ablesbar an allen im Laufe der Jahrhunderte entstandenen Bauten, die geschmiedete Architekturteile aufweisen. Es handelt sich darum, jeweils die passende Formgebung für das Eisen zu finden und die Gestaltungsformen zu variieren. Einfühlung in das Althergebrachte ist ebenso wichtig wie auf der anderen Seite der kühne Sprung in künstlerisches Neuland. Dabei darf der Kunstschmied nie vergessen, das besondere eigene Leben seines Materials spürbar werden zu lassen. Nur wenn ihm das gelungen ist, wird auch die Formgebung und Gestaltung fehlerfrei sein. Verwendungszwecke, Aufstellungsort, besondere Gegebenheiten der Umwelt müssen berücksichtigt werden in Komposition und Abwandlung der Formen. Wesentlich ist die sorgfältige Ausführung des kleinsten Details, das zur Harmonie des Ganzen beiträgt. Ich bin der Meinung, daß hier wie überall die Natur die beste Lehrmeisterin ist. Wo gibt es sonst diese unerschöpfliche Vielfalt der Formen? Man muß sie nur erkennen und übertragen. Das soll nicht heißen, man müßte auf die eigene Phantasie verzichten. Allerdings wird es immer wieder vorkommen, daß Zweck und besondere Umstände eines Auftrags die freie, schöpferische Gestaltung einschränken, denn auf gewisse Gegebenheiten hat man keinen Einfluß.

Bei der Auswahl der Zeichnungen und Photographien für dies Buch habe ich unterstellt, daß der Leser das ABC des Schmiedens bereits erlernt hat und die Grundvoraussetzungen zu erfüllen schon in der Lage ist. Über diese gebe ich nur indirekt Auskunft. Wohl habe ich bewußt viele Details herausgezeichnet, die sowohl dem berufenen Kunstschmied wie auch dem, der die Kunst erst erlernen will, die nötige Hilfe geben. Meiner Ansicht nach ist vielleicht das Faszinierendste an unserem spröden Material die Tatsache, daß man ihm so vielfältige Formen verleihen kann. Unentbehrlich für die künstlerische und auch die rein handwerkliche Arbeit sind, wie ich aus jahrelanger Erfahrung weiß und immer wieder betonen möchte, die exakten, maßstabgerechten Zeichnungen. Das ist die Grundlage. Ich habe häufig beobachtet, wie viele Meister in ihrer Werkstatt die Bedeutung der zeichnerischen Festlegung unterschätzen, ja gering achten. Allzuoft wird da improvisiert, flüchtig auf Holz oder Blechtafeln oder auch nur mit Kreide auf den Fußboden eine Zeichnung hingeworfen. Dann ist das gute Gelingen mehr oder weniger eine Frage des Zufalls.

Der rechte Weg, den ich immer beschritten habe, ist hier eine genaue Naturskizze im Maßstab des anzufertigenden Werkstücks auf Packpapier zu zeichnen und damit alle Details getreu festzuhalten. Das bedeutet einen weiteren, großen Vorteil: den der wirtschaftlichen Anfertigung und der Möglichkeit, die Zeichnungen zu archivieren, um sie für spätere neue Aufträge zur Hand zu haben und auch Kunden vorzulegen, die eine Bestellung aufgeben möchten. Dieser Methode verdanke ich mein in die Tausende gehendes Archiv von Werkzeichnungen, die, nach Gegenständen geordnet und mit Modellnummern versehen, jederzeit greifbar sind.

6

Die hier wiedergegebenen Zeichnungen von Werkstücken sind alle von mir entworfen und original, wie ich sie meinen Kunstschmieden zur Ausführung vorgelegt habe. Damit waren sie in der Lage, das von ihnen geformte Eisen stets mit der Zeichnung zu vergleichen und, wenn notwendig, Korrekturen vorzunehmen.

7

In meiner jahrzehntelangen Tätigkeit als Kunstschmied habe ich die Erfahrung gemacht, daß Kunden sich nur äußerst selten für abstrakte Formen entscheiden, wenn es um die Gestaltung ihrer unmittelbaren häuslichen Umgebung geht. Denn in ihrem Heim möchten sie einen ruhenden Pol für ihren inneren Menschen schaffen, das allzu Moderne abstreifen und sich die Mühe des „Fortschrittlichen" ersparen, weil sie nicht Spannung und Aufregung, sondern Muße und friedliche Schönheit der Form suchen. Ich glaube, die „abstrakte Linie" bringt dem Handwerker wenig geschäftlichen Nutzen. Dabei räume ich gern ein, daß hier jeder seine eigenen Erfahrungen machen mag.

Es soll mit dieser Feststellung nicht behauptet werden, daß der Kunstschmied sich dem Geist der Gegenwart verschließen müßte, weil sein Handwerk ein so altes, ehrwürdiges ist. Die Kunst liegt auch in der Fähigkeit, Altes mit Neuem zu verbinden.

Mein besonderes Anliegen besteht darin, Interesse und Verständnis für die Schmiedekunst erneut zu wecken. Ich hoffe und glaube, dies sei

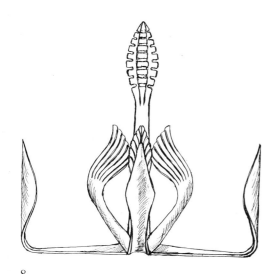

8

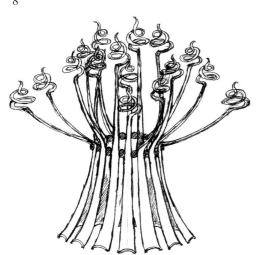

9

10

mir bereits in meinem schon erschienenen ersten Buch gelungen. Wohl habe ich bereits mit Zeichnungen und Photographien die Kunstschmiedearbeiten am Bau behandelt, doch gebe ich hier ganz bewußt und gezielt Anregungen und im weiteren Sinne Anleitungen zur Formenfindung. Dem schönen Handwerk der Schmiedekunst zu dienen, war meine Lebensaufgabe, das Erlernte und Ausgeübte weiterzugeben, entspricht meiner innersten Überzeugung. Denn die Weitergabe von Generation zu Generation prägt die Eigenart unseres Handwerks. In diesem Sinne habe ich mich bemüht, meine Gedanken in dem vorliegenden Buch zum Ausdruck zu bringen. Heute, da meine Werkstatt im Herzen Wiens geschlossen ist und zu einem Museum wurde, erstreckt sich meine Tätigkeit als schöpferischer Kunstschmied auf die Arbeit am Zeichentisch und nicht mehr am Amboß. Und aus meinem Studio gehen immer noch viele neue Entwürfe in die Welt hinaus. Denn „im Eisen" denken und die Vorstellung zu Papier bringen – das ist ohnehin ein Vorgang, der ablaufen muß, ehe man vor dem Amboß stehen kann. Jede andere Reihenfolge wäre verkehrt. Ich möchte meine Vorrede mit einem Ausspruch von Heinz Quilitzsch schließen, der zur Eisenkunst so gut paßt und mir besonders viel sagt:

„Die künstlerische Aufgabe erfüllt sich nicht allein in der Gestaltung des schöpferischen Werkes, sondern erhält ihren eigentlichen Wert erst durch die Wirkung auf den Beschauer."

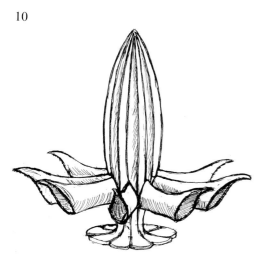

Geschmiedete Bildwerke

Unter diesem Begriff werden hier sowohl Einzelstücke als auch Teile eines Ganzen verstanden, die ein eigenes kleines Bildwerk darstellen, das ohne praktischen Zweck oder besondere Funktion in sich selbst beschlossen ist. In unseren Beispielen, Abb. 1–28, zeigt sich, wie in der Gestaltung durchaus der Phantasie freier Lauf gelassen werden darf. Anlehnungen an die Natur sind ebenso gefällig und gefragt wie abstrakte Gebilde, eine Ausbreitung in der Fläche ebenso wie das Hineinragen in den Raum in allen Richtungen. Auf diese Weise läßt sich auch nach Belieben eine moderne Linienführung im Sinne der zeitgenössischen Kunst verwirklichen, gleichsam um zu beweisen, daß die Designer in der Schmiedekunst es sehr wohl mit den Designern aufnehmen können, die sich auf anderen Gebieten hervortun. Wer es sich zutraut, mache einmal einen solchen Versuch.

Abb. 3. Geschmiedetes Schlosserwappen.
Abb. 6–11, 13, 14, 19–22. Diese geschmiedeten Bildwerke verdeutlichen, was oben zu dem Hineinragen in den Raum gesagt wurde.
Abb. 4, 5, 12, 15, 16, 18, 26–28. Hier muß der Kunstschmied sein besonderes Augenmerk auf die Flächenausbildung richten. Ein großer Teil dieser Arbeiten hat ja flächenfüllenden Charakter.
Abb. 15, 17, 23–25. Als Mittelmotive bieten sich vor allem rundplastische Figuren an.

Preface

12

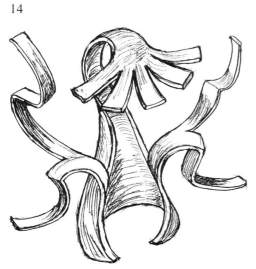

13

14

The subject that I have chosen for this book is ironwork for buildings, past and present. Wrought ironwork on a building has the double function of protection and ornamentation, and here both functions will be emphasized. This twofold purpose presents the creative handicraftsman with many different tasks, because work in architectural context requires both a special talent for adapting and a feeling for very subtle variations. All buildings with wrought ironwork give evidence of this. In each case it is a question of finding the appropriate design for the iron and of varying the way it is worked. A feeling for traditional forms is just as important as the daring raid into new artistic territory. In this process the wrought-iron craftsman must never neglect to evoke the unique nature of his material. Only when he manages this will both the design and the workmanship be perfect. The function of the work, its location, and special factors in the environment must be taken into consideration in the composition and variation of the forms. Of primary importance is the painstaking workmanship of even the smallest detail, for it contributes to the harmony of the whole. I believe that here, as everywhere, Nature is the best teacher.

Where else can such an inexhaustible variety of forms be found? One need only recognize and transform them, though this does not mean renouncing one's own creative imagination. However, since the craftsman has no overriding control, it occurs constantly that the purpose and the special conditions of a commission are for ever setting limits on a free, creative design.

When making selection of drawings and photographs for this book I assumed that the reader has already learned the ABC of forging iron, and possesses basic knowledge. I deal only indirectly with these elements. I do, however, consciously provide many details that can help both the qualified wrought-iron craftsman and someone who wishes to begin learning the trade. In my opinion, perhaps the most fascinating thing about our unyielding material is the fact that one can impart to it such a variety of forms. Indispensable for both the creative and the purely mechanical work are exact, true-to-scale drawings, as I know from years of experience, and always like to emphasize again and again.

These are the basis. I have frequently observed master craftsmen in their workshops who undervalue, even make light of, the importance of a precise delineation. All too often one improvises, one tosses off a drawing on wood or on a metal sheet, or sometimes simply with chalk on the floor. Then success is more or less a question of chance.

The best method, which I have always followed, is to draw on packing paper an exact, full-size sketch, on the scale of the piece to be made. Thus all details are faithfully recorded on paper. This brings a further big advantage, that of economical production, and also the possibility of filing away the drawings, in order to have them at hand for new commissions in the future, and for display to clients who would like to place an order. As a result of this method, I have an archive of working drawings that run into the thousands and which, ordered according to subjects and provided with pattern numbers, are always within reach.

15

The drawings of pieces reproduced here are all original and sketched by me, as I gave them to my wrought-iron craftsmen for execution. Thus the men were in a position constantly to compare the iron which they had forged with my drawing, and when necessary to undertake corrective measures.

In my experience as wrought-iron craftsman over several decades, I have found that clients only very rarely choose abstract forms where the furnishing of their immediate domestic surroundings is concerned. In their homes they would like to create a tranquil environment, by ridding themselves of an all too modern style, and by sparing themselves the effort of the 'progressive'. What they seek is not tension and agitation but rather a leisurely atmosphere and a peaceful beauty of form. In my view, the 'abstract style' is of little commercial benefit to the craftsman, although I grant that others may have different experience here. However, I dot not intend to claim that the wrought-iron craftsman must cut himself off from the spirit of the present because his craft is such a venerable one. The art of ironwork also lies in the ability to unite old and new.

What I would like to do in particular is to reawaken interest in, and understanding for, the art of wrought ironwork. I hope and believe that this has already been achieved in my first published book (Der Kunstschmied Otto Schmirler, Wasmuth 1977). It is true that I have already dealt with wrought ironwork for buildings by means of drawings and photographs, but in this book I consciously and intentionally give

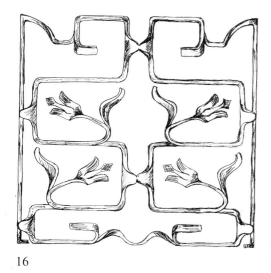

16

17

18

suggestions, and in a sense directions, for developing a form. To devote myself to the beautiful craftsmanship of wrought-iron art has been my life's work; to pass on what has been learned and proven has been my guiding principle. For the very essence of our craft is the handing down of experience from generation to generation, and for that reason I have tried to express my thoughts in this book. At the present time, because my shop in the centre of Vienna has been closed and has become a museum, my activity as a creative wrought-iron craftsman is confined to work at the drawing table, and no longer includes that on the anvil. Yet from my studio many new designs still go out into the world, for to think 'in iron' and to embody the idea on paper is in any case a process that must be completed before one may stand in front of the anvil. Any other order would be mistaken. I would like to end my preface with the words of Heinz Quilitzsch, which fit wrought ironwork so well, and mean very much to me:

The task of the artist is not fulfilled simply in the creation of a work, for it only receives its true value through the effect on the observer.

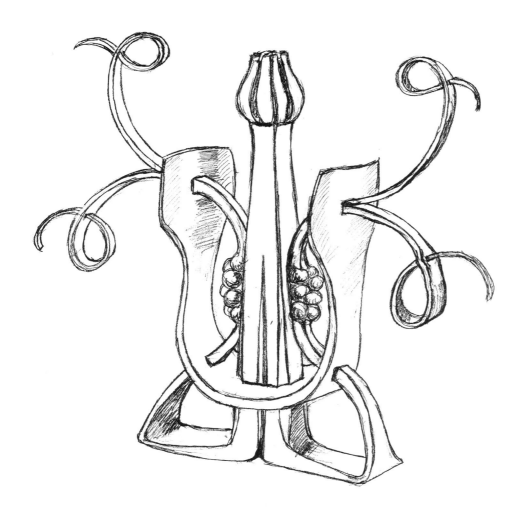

Wrought Sculptures

This term covers individual pieces as well as parts of a whole which present a small, self-contained sculpture having no practical function or special purpose. Our examples, Ill. 1–28, show that the imagination may certainly be given free play in design. Imitations of nature are just as attractive as abstract figures, and are requested just as often; the same is true of the spread of a surface area or a projection into the room in all directions. In this way, if one prefers, a modern style as in contemporary art can also be used to advantage, to prove as it were that the designers in the wrought-iron craft are more than a match for those designers who have distinguished themselves in other areas. Whoever has enough confidence in his abilities can make such an attempt.

Ill. 3. The locksmith's blazonry in wrought-iron.
Ill. 6–11, 13, 14, 19–22. These wrought sculptures demonstrate what was said above about projection into the room.
Ill. 4, 5, 12, 15, 16, 18, 26–28. Here the wrought-iron craftsman has to concentrate on the development of a surface area. It is in the nature of many of these works to fill in such an area.
Ill. 15, 17, 23–5. Sculptural figures are especially fitting as a central motif.

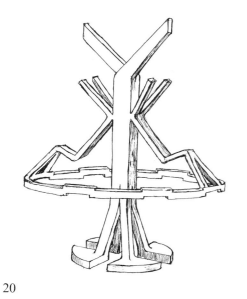

20

21

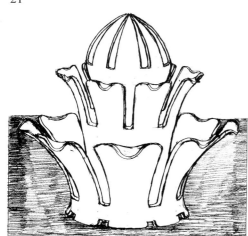

22

Préface

Le sujet que j'ai choisi pour ce livre est l'art du fer forgé dans la maison et le jardin, hier et aujourd'hui. Le fer forgé dans la maison a deux fonctions: protéger et décorer. Ces deux fonctions doivent être mises ici en valeur. Il en résulte de multiples tâches pour l'ouvrier à l'esprit créateur. Car l'architecture suppose une faculté d'adaptation bien particulière, ainsi que le sens des modifications subtiles. On s'en rend compte en considérant, au cours des siècles, toutes les constructions qui présentent des parties forgées. Il s'agit à chaque fois de trouver la forme qui convient pour le fer et de varier le façonnage. Il est tout aussi important pour l'artisan de savoir s'identifier au traditionnel que d'oser s'aventurer dans un domaine artistique nouveau. Le ferronnier d'art ne doit cependant jamais oublier de faire sentir la vie propre et particulière de son matériau. La forme et la façon ne seront parfaites que s'il y parvient. L'utilisation, le lieu de mise en place, les données particulières de l'environnement sont des facteurs à considérer lors de la composition et de la modification des formes. L'essentiel est l'exécution minutieuse du plus petit détail qui contribue à l'harmonie de l'ensemble. Je pense qu'ici comme partout ailleurs c'est la nature qui sert de modèle. Où trouve-t-on, sinon dans la nature, cette diversité inépuisable des formes? Il suffit de les reconnaître et de les transposer.

Ce qui ne veut pas dire qu'il faille renoncer à sa propre imagination et fantaisie. Bien entendu, il arrive toujours que l'imagination créatrice soit limitée par le but et les circonstances particulières d'une commande, car il y a des données qu'on ne peut pas manipuler à son gré.

En choisissant les dessins et photographies pour ce livre, j'ai supposé que le lecteur a déjà appris l'ABC de cet art du fer forgé et qu'il est en mesure de remplir les conditions fondamentales nécessaires à cette connaissance. Je n'en parle donc qu'indirectement. C'est intentionnellement que j'ai dessiné de nombreux détails qui apporteront l'aide nécessaire aussi bien au ferronnier d'art compétent qu'à celui qui veut d'abord apprendre cet art. A mon avis, ce que notre matériau peu souple a de plus fascinant, c'est le fait qu'on peut lui prêter de multiples formes. Après des années d'expérience, je sais – et j'aimerais insister sur ce fait – que des dessins exacts faits à l'échelle sont indispensables pour le travail artistique et pour le travail purement artisanal. C'est la base en somme. J'ai souvent constaté que de nombreux maîtres sous-estiment et même dédaigent la signification du dessin. Trop souvent on improvise, on trace rapidement un dessin sur du bois ou de la tôle, ou même à la craie sur le plancher. Le résultat n'est alors plus ou moins qu'une question de hasard.

La seule façon – qui fut toujours la mienne – est de faire une esquisse exacte sur papier d'emballage, à l'échelle de l'ouvrage à réaliser, en fixant ainsi tous les détails. Ceci représente d'autres avantages: une fabrication économique et la possibilité de conserver les dessins afin de les avoir plus tard sous la main pour les présenter à d'éventuels clients qui veulent passer une commande. Grâce à cette méthode, je me suis constitué des archives comptant des milliers de dessins classés par objets, numérotés et accessibles à tout instant.

23

Les dessins d'ouvrages reproduits ici sont tous des originaux de ma main, tels que je les ai remis à mes ferronniers d'art. Ainsi, ils pouvaient toujours comparer leur travail en cours d'exécution au dessin et pourvoir à d'éventuelles corrections. Au cours des nombreuses années de mon activité professionnelle en tant que ferronnier d'art j'ai constaté que les clients ne souhaitaient que très rarement des formes abstraites pour l'aménagement de leur milieu domestique. Dans leur maison ils désirent trouver un endroit reposant, dépouillé de trop de modernisme et d'avant-gardisme, car ils recherchent la détente et la beauté paisible des formes et non pas la tension et l'agitation. Je crois que la «ligne abstraite» représente peu d'intérêt commercial pour l'artisan. Cependant j'admets qu'ici chacun doit faire sa propre expérience.

24

25

Cette constatation ne doit pas nous amener à affirmer que le ferronnier d'art doive se fermer à tout esprit moderne et ce parce que son métier est ancien et vénérable. L'art consiste également à combiner l'ancien et le moderne.

Mon désir est d'éveiller de nouveau l'intérêt et la compréhension pour l'art du fer forgé. J'espère et je crois y être parvenu avec mon premier livre. J'ai déjà traité le travail de la ferronnerie d'art dans le bâtiment avec des dessins et des photographies, mais je voudrais donner ici, sciemment, des impulsions et au sens plus large des instructions pour la recherche du façonnage. La tâche de toute ma vie a été de servir le beau métier de la ferronnerie d'art; ma profonde conviction a été de devoir transmettre ce que j'avais appris et pratiqué. Car la transmission de génération en génération est la particularité de notre profession.

26

C'est dans ce sens que je me suis efforcé d'exprimer mes pensées dans ce livre. Aujourd'hui, alors que ma forge au cœur de Vienne est fermée et est devenue un musée, mon activité en tant que ferronnier d'art s'exerce à la planche à dessiner et non plus à l'enclume. Et de nombreuses ébauches nouvelles quittent encore mon studio. Car penser «en fer» et réaliser «sur papier» c'est un processus qui doit se dérouler avant que l'on puisse se mettre à l'enclume. Tout autre ordre de succession des choses serait faux. J'aimerais terminer mon introduction par une déclaration de Heinz Quilitzsch qui convient très bien à la ferronnerie d'art et qui me paraît particulièrement importante:

«La tâche artistique ne s'accomplit pas seulement dans le façonnage de l'œuvre créatrice; elle ne reçoit sa valeur réelle qu'à travers l'impression exercée sur le spectateur.»

27

Œuvres d'art forgées

On entend par là aussi bien des pièces individuelles que des parties d'un ensemble qui représentent une petite œuvre d'art propre et complète, sans but pratique et sans fonction particulière. Nos reproductions 1–28 montrent comment on peut laisser libre cours à l'imagination dans le façonnage. Des emprunts à la nature sont tout aussi demandés et appréciés que des œuvres abstraites, un élargissement de la surface aussi bien que des saillies dans toutes les directions. De cette façon on peut réaliser à volonté une forme moderne dans le sens de l'art contemporain, pour prouver en quelque sorte que les «designers» de la ferronnerie d'art peuvent se mesurer avec ceux qui se distinguent dans d'autres domaines. Que celui qui s'en croit capable, en fasse l'essai.

Fig. 3. Blason des serruriers en fer forgé.
Fig. 6–11, 13, 14, 19–22: ces œuvres d'art forgées montrent en clair ce qui a été dit plus haut à propos des saillies dans l'espace.
Fig. 4, 5, 12, 15, 16, 18, 26–28: ici le ferronnier d'art doit avoir en vue le développement de la surface. Une grande partie de ces travaux est consacrée au remplissage de la surface.
Fig. 15, 17, 23–25: des figures plastiques rondes conviennent en tant que motifs centraux.

29

Gartentore

Entscheidend für den ersten Eindruck der Schmiedekunst am Haus ist zunächst das Gartentor, durch
welches man eintritt. Je nach Wunsch des Auftragge-
bers wird der Kunstschmied das Tor ein- oder zwei-
flüglig gestalten oder aber ein Einfahrtstor mit Gehtüre kombiniert ausführen. Bei den Entwürfen für
das Tor ist es von entscheidender Bedeutung, sie
dem Gebäude und seiner Architektur anzupassen,
weil das Tor ja dorthin leitet.
Abb. 32, 33, 64, 67. Gartentorrahmen aus Stahlpro-
filen haben den Vorzug, zugleich massiver zu wirken
und doch im Gewicht leichter zu sein. Oft genügt
wenig geschmiedeter Dekor, um das Tor harmonisch
und schön zu gestalten.
Abb. 30, 31, 39, 40, 65. Es ist durchaus vertretbar,
das gleiche Motiv für die Gehtüre, das Garagentor
und auch das Zaungitter zu verwenden.
Abb. 56, 57, 49. Besonders bei größeren Entfernun-
gen zum Haus empfiehlt sich der Einbau eines elek-
trischen Türöffners.
Abb. 43 und 46. Das Einfahrtstor mit je einer Gehtüre rechts und links bildet ein geschlossenes Gan-
zes.
Abb. 75. Als Hintergrund des Gartentores wurde
Rohgußglas verwendet. Es bildet einen guten Kon-
trast zum Gitterwerk und erscheint optisch als Fort-
setzung der Mauerfläche.

Garden Gates

The front gate of a house is crucial for one's first impression of its wrought ironwork. Depending on
the client's wishes, the wrought-iron craftsman can
construct either a single or a double gate, or a
combination of gates for driveway and footpath.
In designing the gate it is of great importance to
match the gate to the building and its architectural
style.
Ill. 32, 33, 64, 67. Garden gate frames of steel sections have the advantage of appearing more solid
and being at the same time lighter in actual weight.
Often only a little wrought decoration is enough
to fashion the gate into a harmonious and attractive
work.
Ill. 30, 31, 39, 40, 65. It is quite acceptable to use
the same motif for the gate, the garage door and
the fence railing.
Ill. 56, 57, 49. Particularly where there are long distances from the gate to the house, the instalment
of an electric door opener is recommended.
Ill. 43 and 46. The entrance gate and the doors to
the right and left form a unified structure.
Ill. 75. Rough-cast glass was used as the background
for this garden gate. It contrasts well with the ironwork and gives the visual impression of being a
continuation of the wall surface.

Portails de jardins

Le portail de jardin donne une impression définitive
de l'art de la ferronnerie dans la construction. Suivant le désir du client, le ferronnier d'art façonnera
un portail à un ou deux battants ou un portail pour
entrée de voiture avec porte d'entrée combinée. Il
est très important, lors des ébauches, d'adapter le
portail au bâtiment et à son architecture, le premier
conduisant au second.
Fig. 32, 33, 64, 67: les encadrements en profil d'acier
du portail de jardin ont l'avantage d'être plus légers
en poids tout en donnant une impression massive.
Il suffit souvent de peu de décoration en fer forgé
pour donner au portail harmonie et beauté.
Fig. 30, 31, 39, 40, 65: on peut très bien utiliser le
même motif pour les portes d'entrée, le portail du
jardin et la grille de clôture.
Fig. 56, 57, 49: lorsque le portail est très éloigné de
la maison, une installation électrique est recomman-
dée.
Fig. 43 et 46: le portail pour entrée de voiture, avec
une porte à droite et à gauche, forme un ensemble
complet.
Fig. 75: comme arrière-plan du portail de jardin on
a utilisé du verre coulé brut. Il offre un contraste
intéressant avec la grille et apparaît optiquement
comme la continuation du mur.

32   195 × 167 cm

33

34 87,5 × 147,5 cm

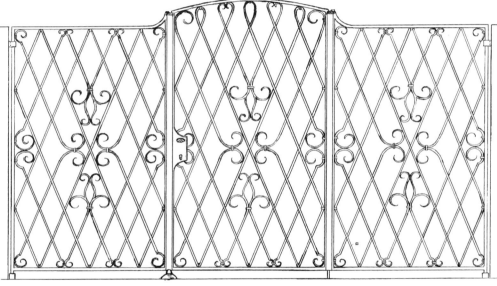

35 330 × 200 cm

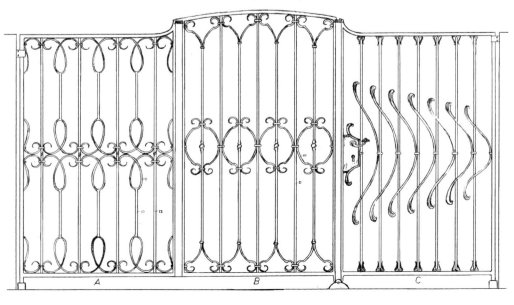

A   B   C

36 330 × 200 cm

37

38　215 × 150 cm

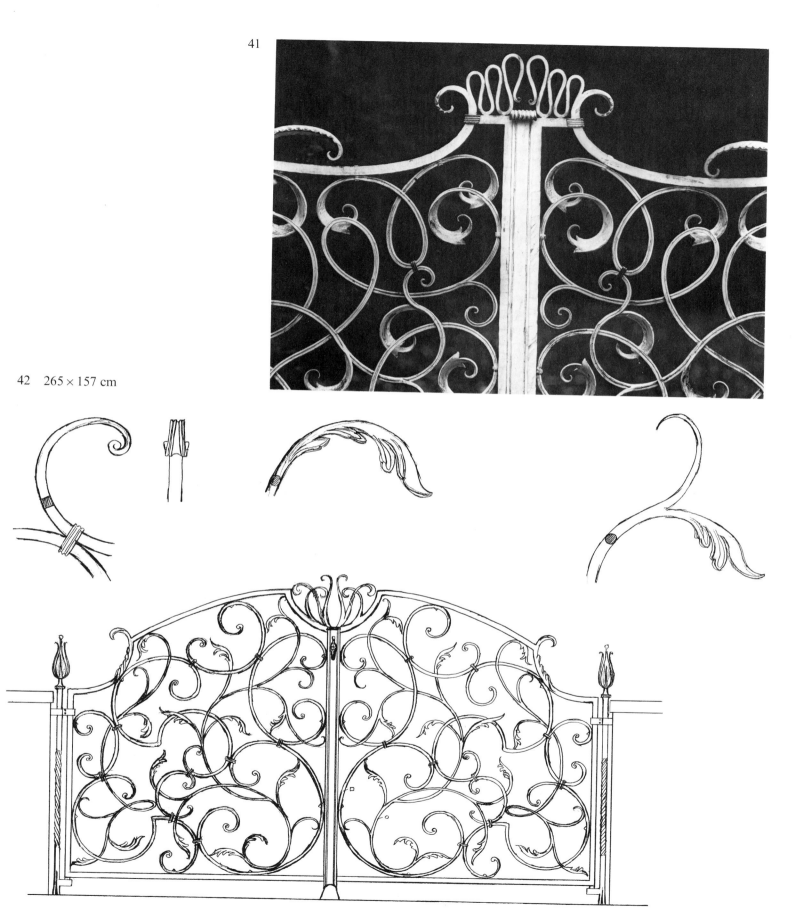

41

42   265 × 157 cm

355 cm

26

43

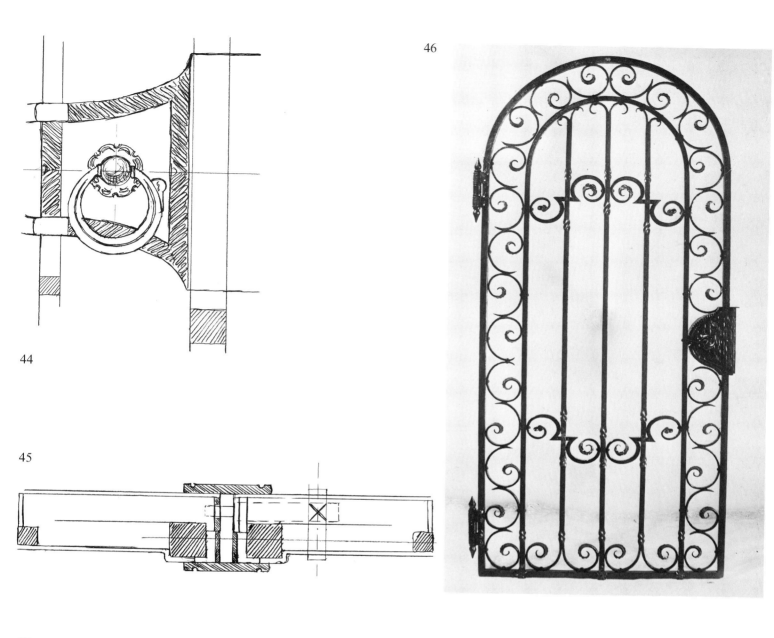

44

45

46

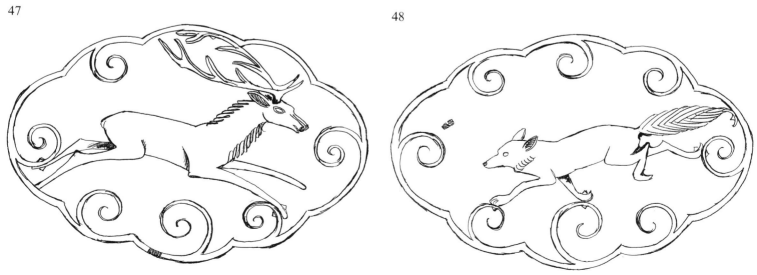

47

48

50

51 97 × 100 cm

52 95 × 115 cm

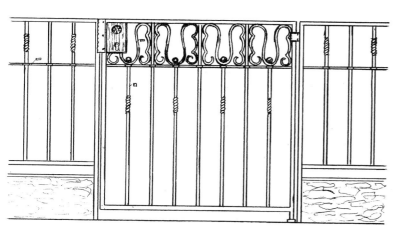

29

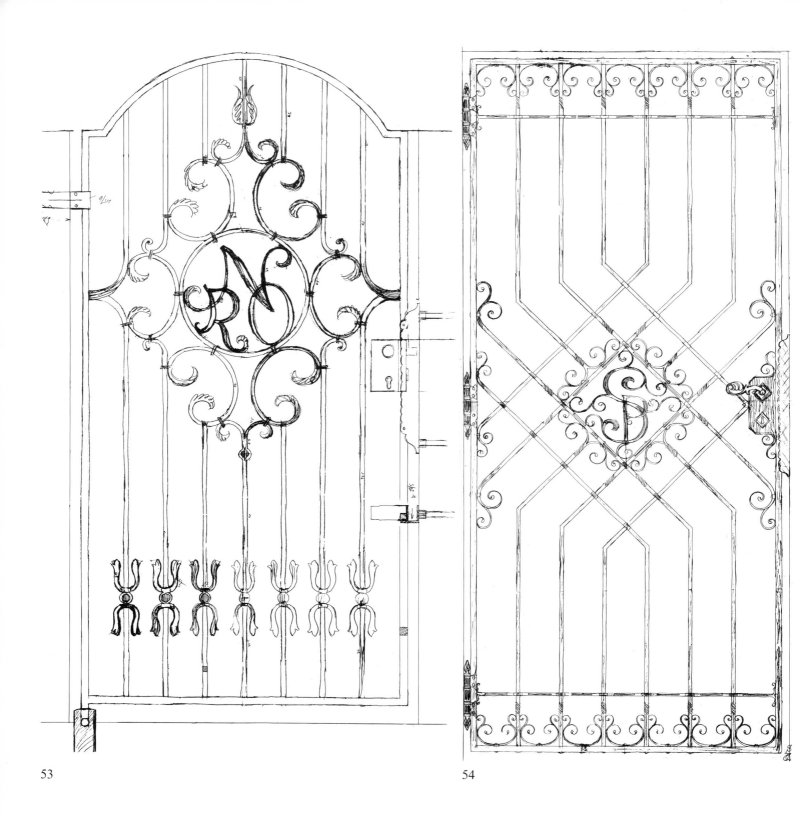

53

54

57

58 122 × 144 cm

20/6

35/7 ▭

12 ⌀

122 cm

18 ▫

22/10 ▭

33

61

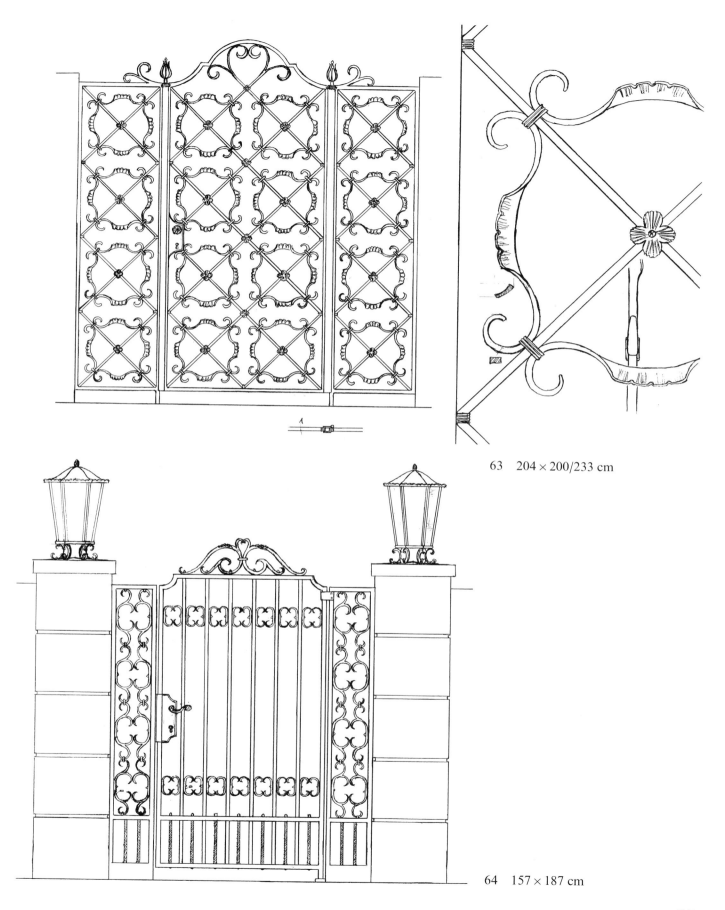

63   204 × 200/233 cm

64   157 × 187 cm

65

66   113 × 165 cm

67   100 × 125 cm

80

81

Briefkasten und Briefeinwurf

An den individuell gefertigten Briefkästen und Briefeinwürfen läßt sich besonders gut ablesen und ermessen, wieviel Liebe zur Sache gerade bei der Kleinarbeit ein Kunstschmied aufwenden muß. In der Praxis wird ein solcher Auftrag wohl immer im Rahmen eines größeren ausgeführt werden – schon aus wirtschaftlichen Überlegungen. Wichtig bei den Briefkästen ist die Warnung, sie ja nicht zu klein anzufertigen und zweitens, für den allerbesten Anstrich zu sorgen, da sie ja dem Wetter ausgesetzt sind. Aus Kupfer gefertigt werden sie am längsten halten.
Abb. 80 und 95. Diese Kästen sind in die Mauer eingelassen.
Abb. 84, 85, 95a. Blechröhren für die Aufnahme von Zeitungen und Zeitschriften.
Abb. 100–106. Bei Briefeinwürfen, die in Gartenpfeilern angebracht sind, läßt sich für den Kasten ein entsprechend großer Raum einplanen.

Letter-boxes and Letter-box Slots

From individually made letter-boxes and slots, one can see and judge how much sheer devotion a craftsman in iron must have to his handiwork, especially to the details. In practice, such work is almost always done as part of a larger commission, of course – if only because of economic considerations. An important warning concerning letter-boxes is, first of all, not to make them too small, and secondly, to provide for the very best coating, since they are exposed to all kinds of weather. Those forged from copper last the longest.
Ill. 80 and 95. These boxes are set into a wall.
Ill. 84, 85, 95a. Sheet-metal tubes for newspaper and magazine delivery.
Ill. 100–6. For letter-box slots that are built into the pillar of a garden wall, a space large enough for the box should be planned.

Boîtes aux lettres

A la façon individuelle dont sont faites les boîtes aux lettres on peut reconnaître et apprécier le talent du ferronnier d'art dans les petits détails. En pratique, ce genre de commande s'effectue toujours dans le cadre d'une commande plus importante, ne serait-ce que pour des raisons économiques. Ce qui est important dans la fabrication des boîtes aux lettres, c'est de ne pas les faire trop petites et de les recouvrir d'une peinture résistant aux intempéries. C'est en cuivre qu'elles résisteront le plus longtemps.
Fig. 80 et 95: ces boîtes sont encastrées dans le mur.
Fig. 84, 85, 95a: tubes en fer blanc pour journaux et revues.
Fig. 100–106: pour les ouvertures des boîtes aux lettres fixées aux piliers du jardin, on doit prévoir assez de place pour la boîte elle-même.

83

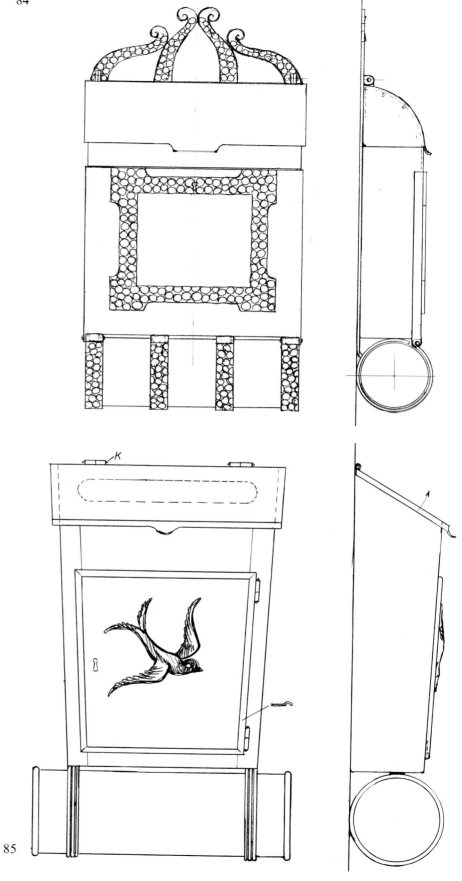

K

85

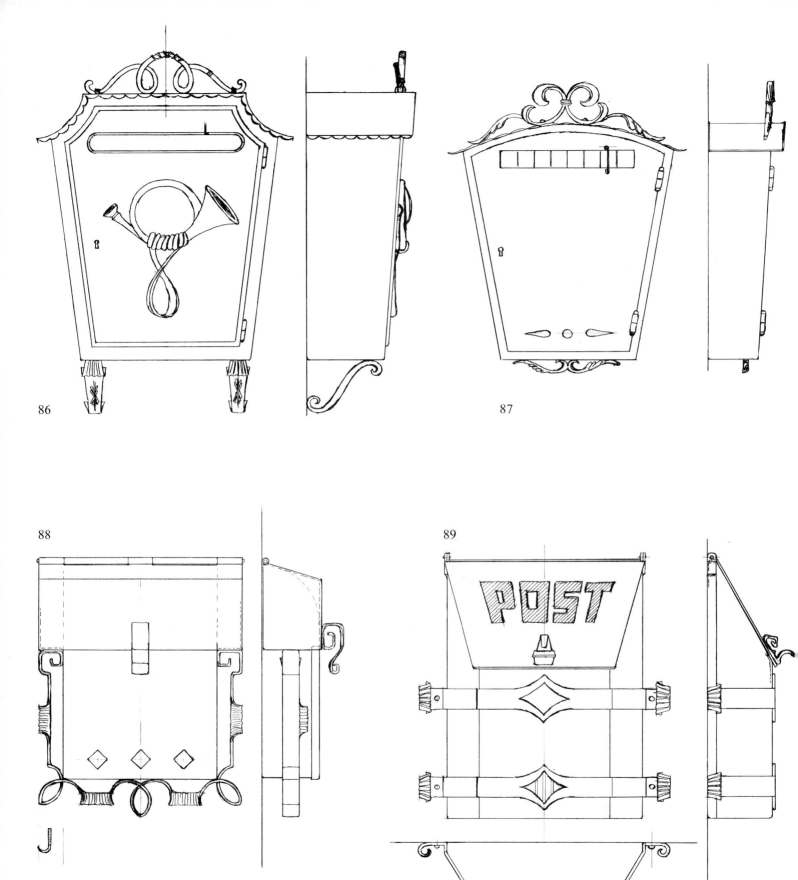

86

87

88

89

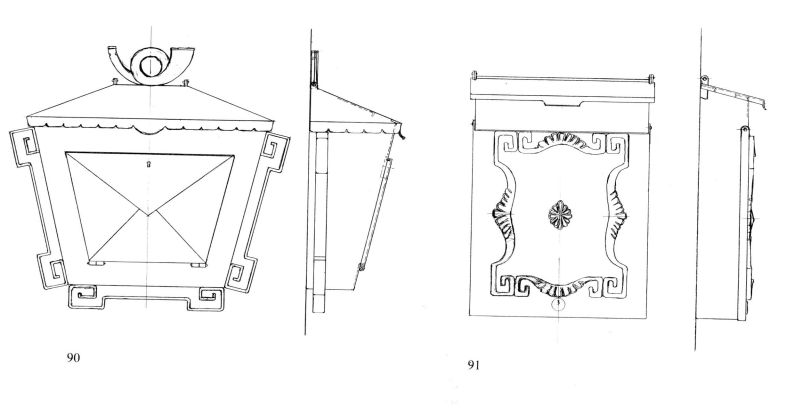

90

91

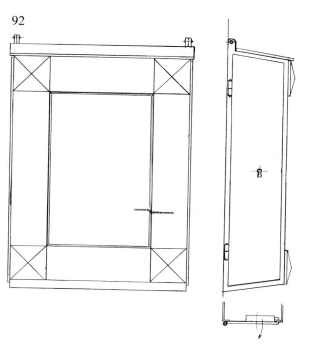

92

93

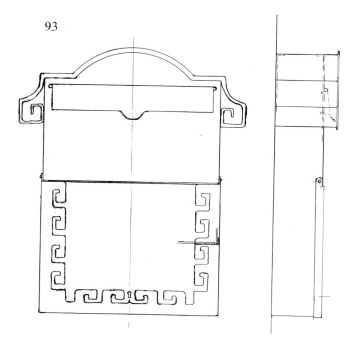

47

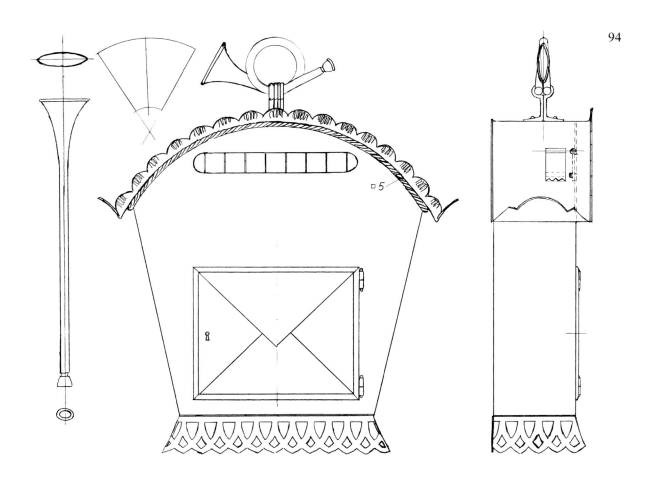

94

□ 5

95

A   B

G

POST

95a

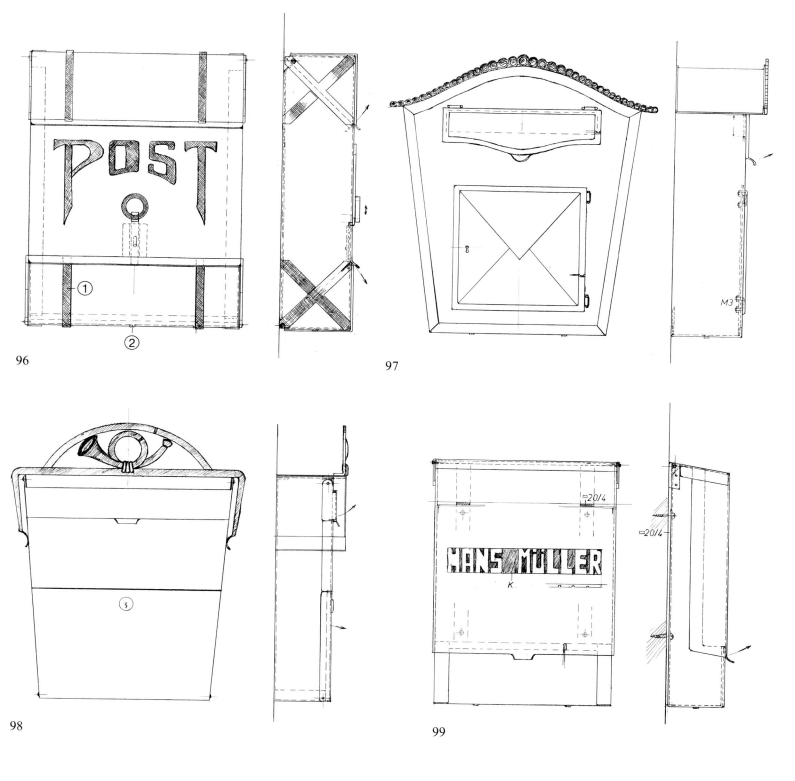

96

97

98

99

① feinkörnig abgehämmert
hammered fine-grained
martelé à grain fin

② Wasserablauf
water discharge
écoulement d'eau

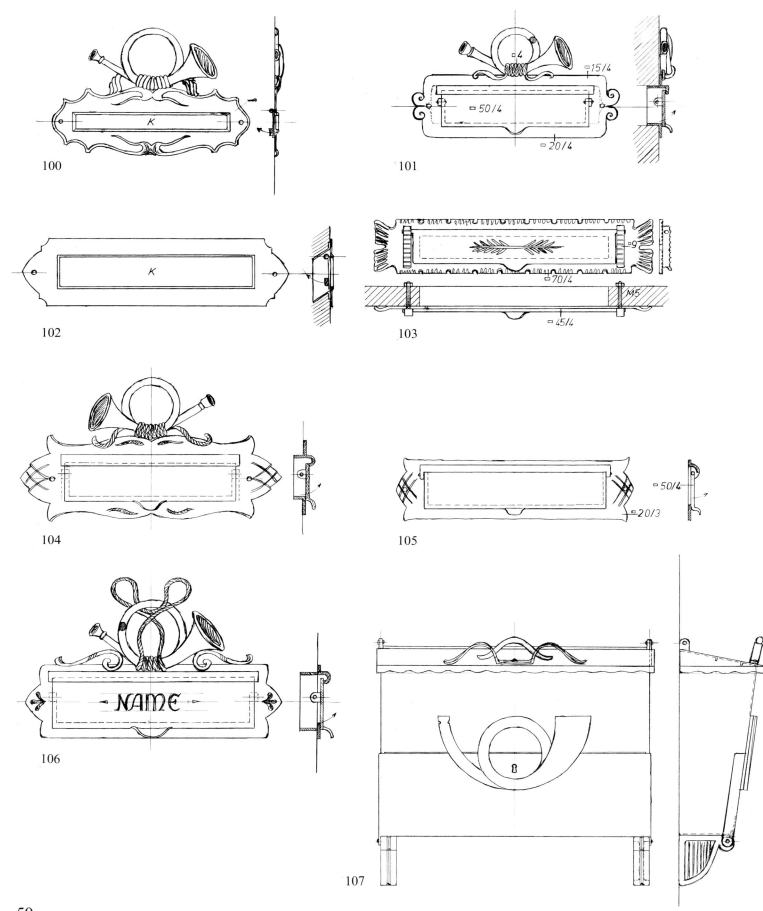

100

101

102

103

104

105

106

107

108

109   240 × 320 cm

Tore und Türen

Künstlerisch geschmiedete Tore und Türen am Haus und im Haus haben verschiedene Funktionen: Sie bilden einen wunderschönen dekorativen Schmuck und bieten gleichzeitig einen Sicherheitsfaktor durch ihren optimalen Verschluß. Über die konstruktiven Lösungen des Türstockes und Türrahmens geben die zahlreichen Werkzeichnungen dieses Abschnitts hinreichend Aufschluß. Die Transparenz des Gitterwerkes ist ein nicht zu unterschätzender Vorteil für die Helligkeit des Raumes. Die Glasfläche mindert diesen Vorteil nicht und bietet außerdem Wärme und Witterungsschutz. Der Farbton und die Oberflächenstruktur des Glases spielen eine Rolle bei der Gestaltung und Vielfältigkeit der Formen.
Abb. 108, 110, 115, 121, 127, 138, 139, 144. Bei großen Raumhöhen ist eine Unterteilung des Gitterwerkes durch ein Oberlicht zweckmäßig. Dadurch erscheint die Tür selbst niedriger und leichter.
Abb. 129, 130, 132–136, 140, 142, 148, 149, 153. In zunehmendem Maße werden heute von der Industrie dem Stahlbauschlosser kalt gewalzte Stahlprofile angeboten und gelangen auch zur Verwendung. Dem Kunstschmied fällt die wichtigere und interessantere Aufgabe zu, für die dekorative Füllung der Fläche zu sorgen. Die einzelnen Werkstätten haben sich in der Praxis eigene Lösungsmethoden erarbeitet. In den von mir angeführten Beispielen wurden Stahlprofile verwendet, die im Vöest-Alpine-Programm enthalten sind. Stets werden auch Walzprofile mitverwendet. – Bei den Türen Abb. 129, 130, 132 und 133 ist das Gitter jeweils vorgesetzt, so daß sich ein Luftflügel zum Öffnen erübrigt. Detail dazu Abb. 134.

Gates and Doors

Artistically wrought gates and doors both outside and inside a house have several functions: they provide a beautiful decoration, and at the same time an element of security. In respect of constructive solutions for the architrave and door-frame, the many working drawings in this section give sufficient information. The fact that light passes through the wrought-iron structure is an advantage that should not be underestimated for the brightness of the room. A glass surface does not take away from this advantage, and offers in addition warmth and protection from the weather. The colour tone and the surface structure of the glass play a part in the design and variety of forms.
Ill. 108, 110, 115, 121, 127, 138, 139, 144. In high-ceilinged rooms, a division of the wrought ironwork with a transom window is practical. As a result the door itself seems to be lower and lighter.
Ill. 129, 130, 132–6, 140, 142, 148, 149, 153. To an increasing degree nowadays industry offers the metal worker cold-rolled steel sections, which are being accepted and used. The wrought-iron craftsman is given the more important and more interesting responsibility of creating the decorative completion of the panel. In practice, the individual shops have worked out their own solutions. For the examples that I present, steel sections available in the Vöest/Alpine series were employed. Rolled sections have also always been used. In each of the doors in Ill. 129, 130, 132 and 133, the wrought ironwork is secured in front of the door, so that a provision for ventilation is no longer necessary, see detail ill. 134.

Portails et portes

Les portails et portes forgés artistiquement (à l'intérieur comme à l'extérieur de la maison) ont différentes fonctions: ils constituent un élément très décoratif et offrent en même temps un facteur optimum de sécurité. Les nombreux dessins de ce chapitre donnent suffisamment d'éclaircissements sur les solutions constructives concernant le montant de la porte et l'huisserie. La transparence de la grille est un avantage considérable pour la clarté de la pièce. La surface en verre ne réduit pas cet avantage, elle apporte en outre chaleur et protection contre les intempéries. La couleur et la structure de la surface du verre jouent également un rôle dans le façonnage et la diversité des formes.
Fig. 108, 110, 115, 121, 127, 138, 139, 144: quand la pièce est très haute, il est recommandé de diviser la grille; la porte apparaît alors plus basse et plus légère.
Fig. 129, 130, 132–136, 140, 142, 148, 149, 153: actuellement, l'industrie propose de plus en plus au serrurier l'utilisation de profilés en fer laminé à froid. C'est au ferronnier d'art que revient la tâche plus importante et plus intéressante de remplir la surface de façon décorative. Les différentes forges ont développé leurs propres méthodes. Dans les exemples que je donne, on a utilisé des profilés contenus dans le programme Vöest-Alpine. On utilise également des profilés laminés.
Pour les portes des figures 129, 130, 132 et 133, la grille est en avant de sorte qu'un vantail est inutile, voir détail fig. 134.

51

110   129 × 278 cm

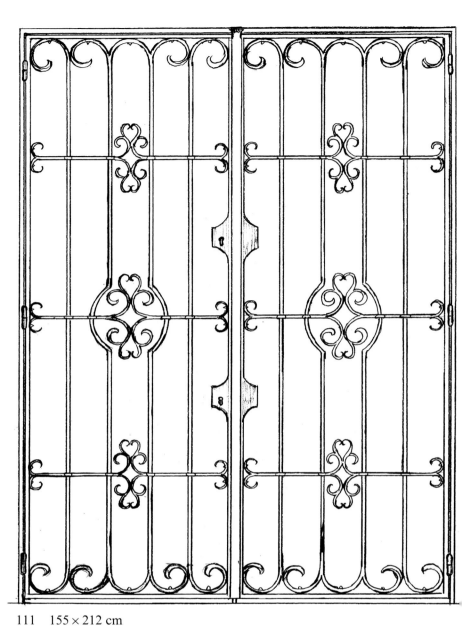

111   155 × 212 cm

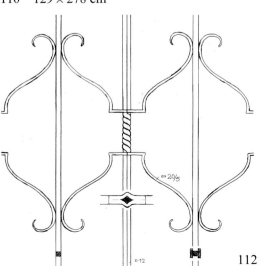

112

113

114   240 × 320 cm

115

116

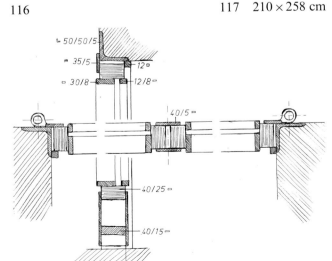

117   210 × 258 cm

54

118

119

55

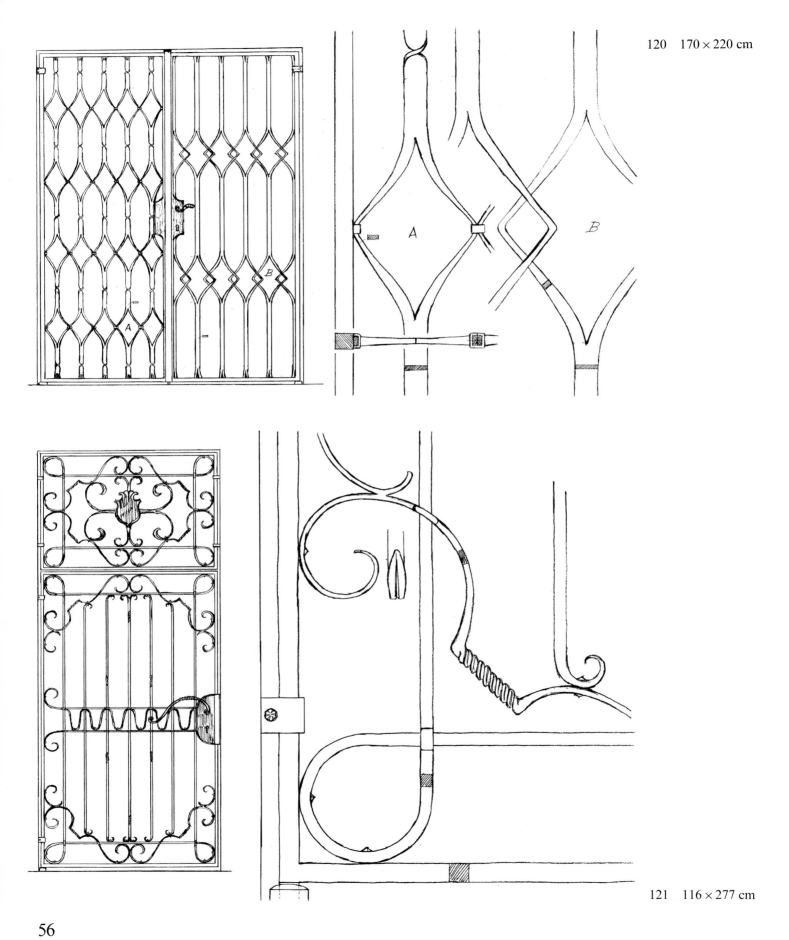

120   170 × 220 cm

121   116 × 277 cm

122   110 × 240 cm

123   136 × 240 cm

Abb. 109–111, 114, 128, 131, 138, 139, 144, 147, 152.
Tore und Türen nur aus Walzprofilen wirken optisch
handwerklicher.
Abb. 115, 116, 138. Hier liegt die Zierfüllung in der
Türfläche, so daß ein Luftflügel zweckmäßig ist.
Bei den Abbildungs-Hinweisen sind zumeist nur
einige Beispiele angeführt.

Ill. 109–11, 114, 128, 131, 138, 139, 144, 147, 152.
Gates and doors fashioned simply from rolled sections give the visual impression of being handcrafted
to a greater extent.
Ill. 115, 116, 138. Because the ornamental work
forms a part of the door surface here, a means of
opening the ironwork for ventilation would be practical.
References to illustrations are usually given in the
more striking cases only.

Fig. 109–111, 114, 128, 131, 138, 139, 144, 147, 152:
portails et portes qui sont seulement en profilés laminés donnent une impression optiquement plus artisa-
nale.
Fig. 115, 116, 138: ici, le remplissage décoratif est
dans la surface de la porte, de sorte qu'un vantail
est nécessaire.
Les références aux illustrations ne comprennent
qu'un certain nombre d'exemples.

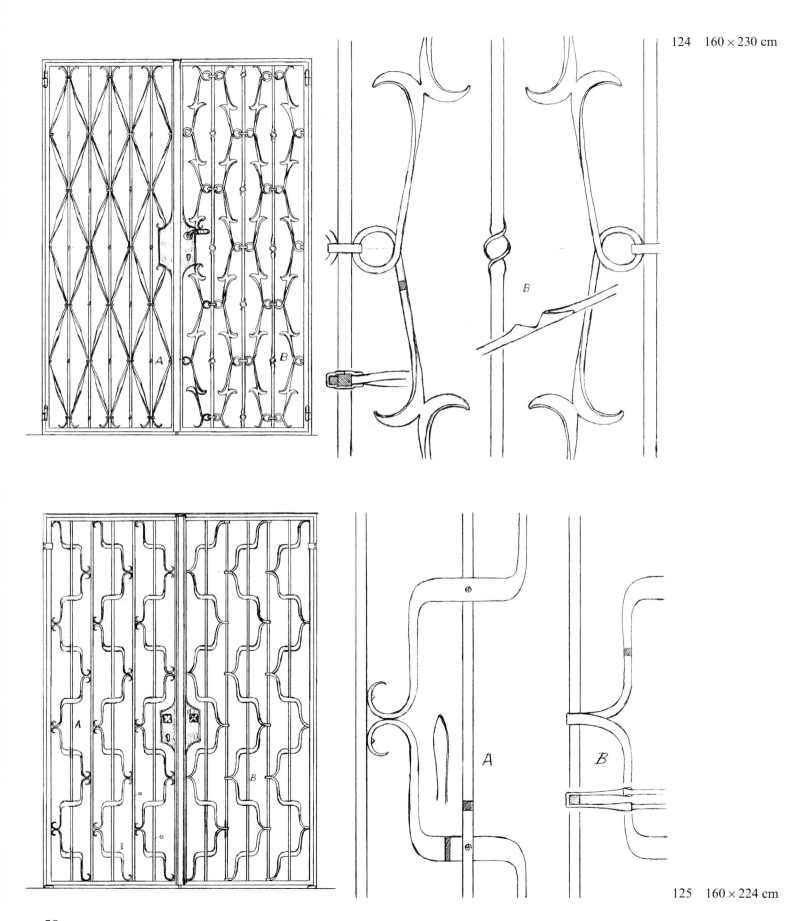

126   125 × 250 cm

127

128　140 × 220 cm

129　100 × 210 cm

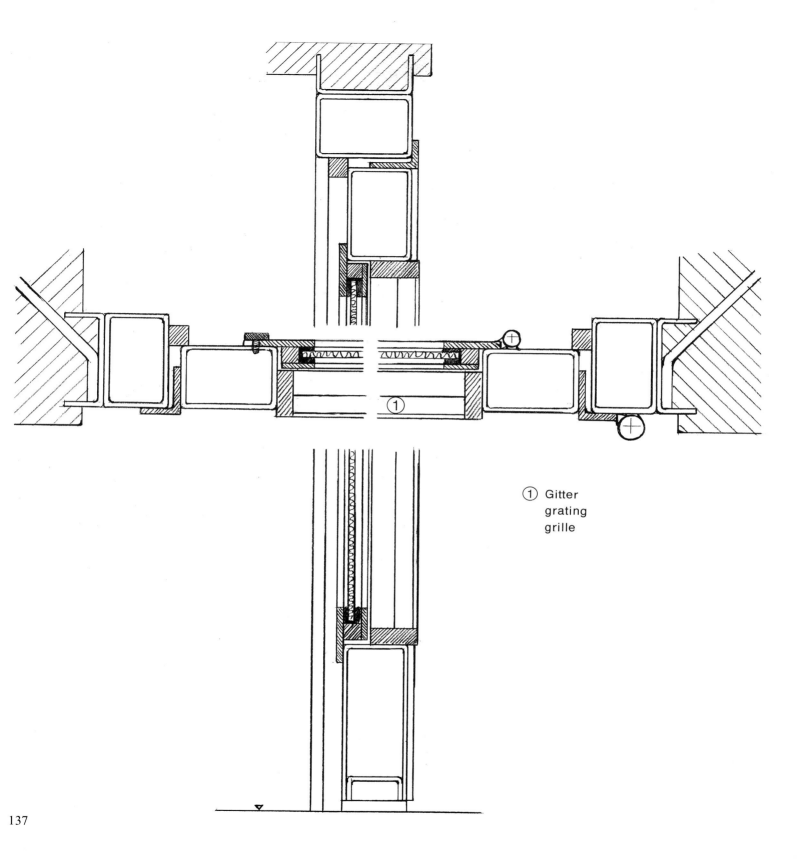

① Gitter
grating
grille

137

65

139

146   110 × 240 cm

147, 148

73

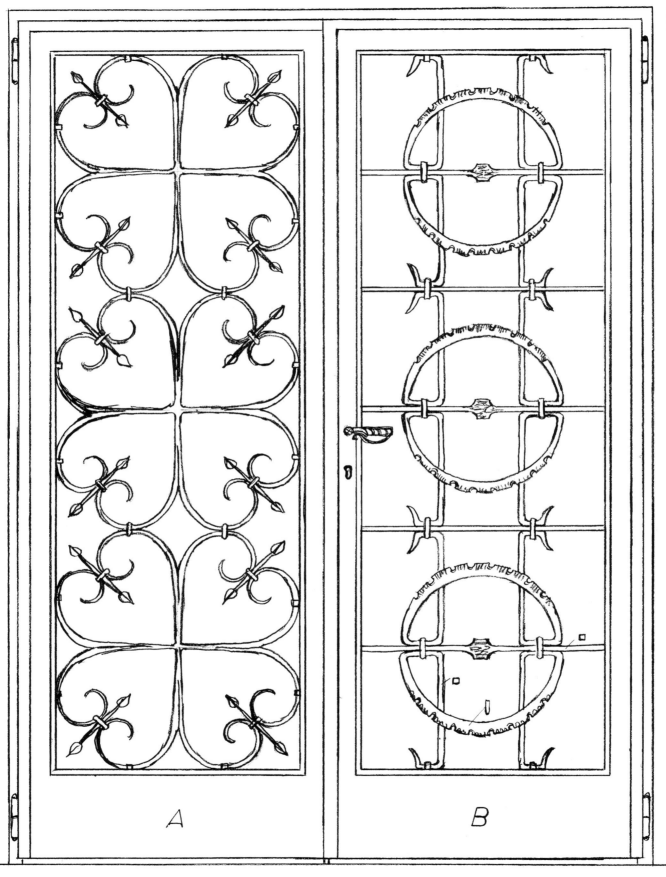

A

B

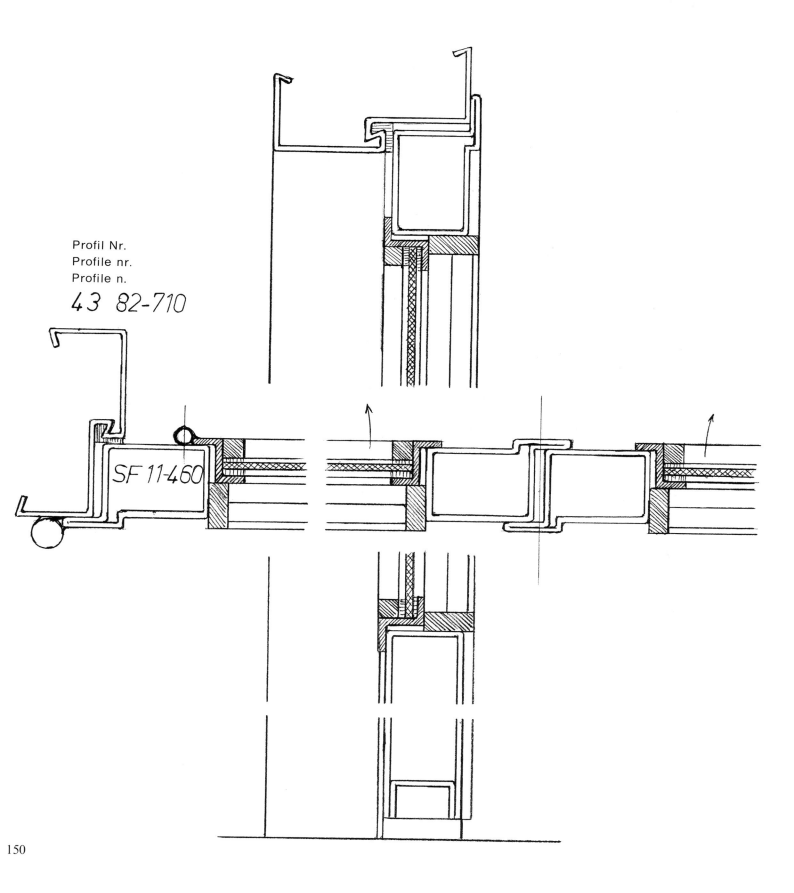

Profil Nr.
Profile nr.
Profile n.

43 82-710

SF 11-460

150

75

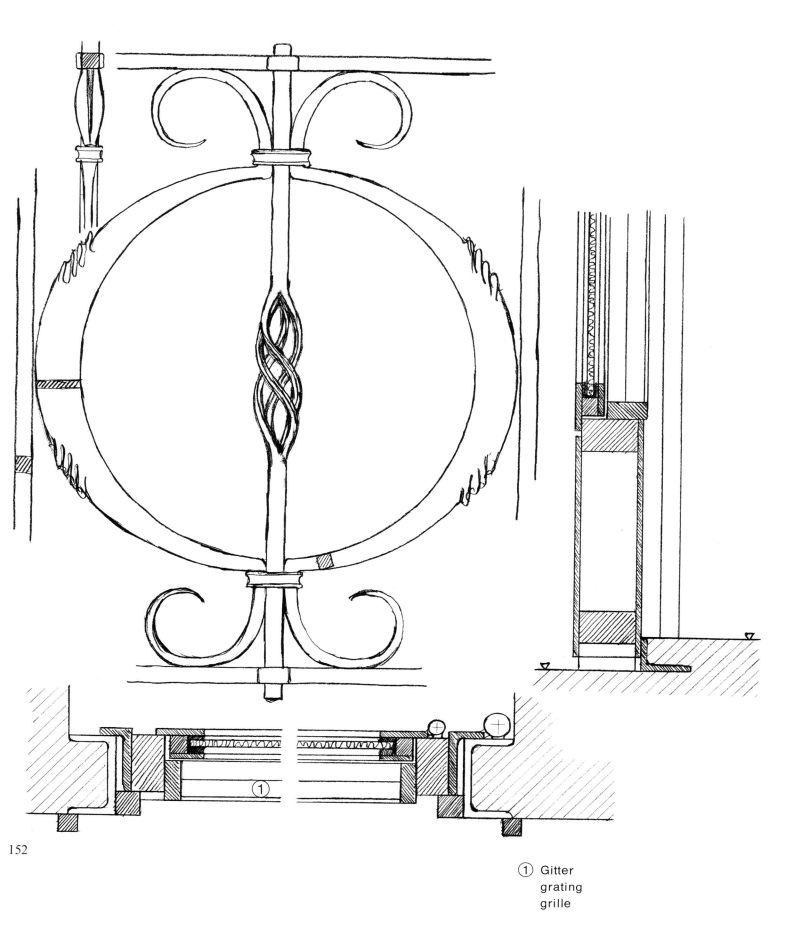

152

① Gitter
grating
grille

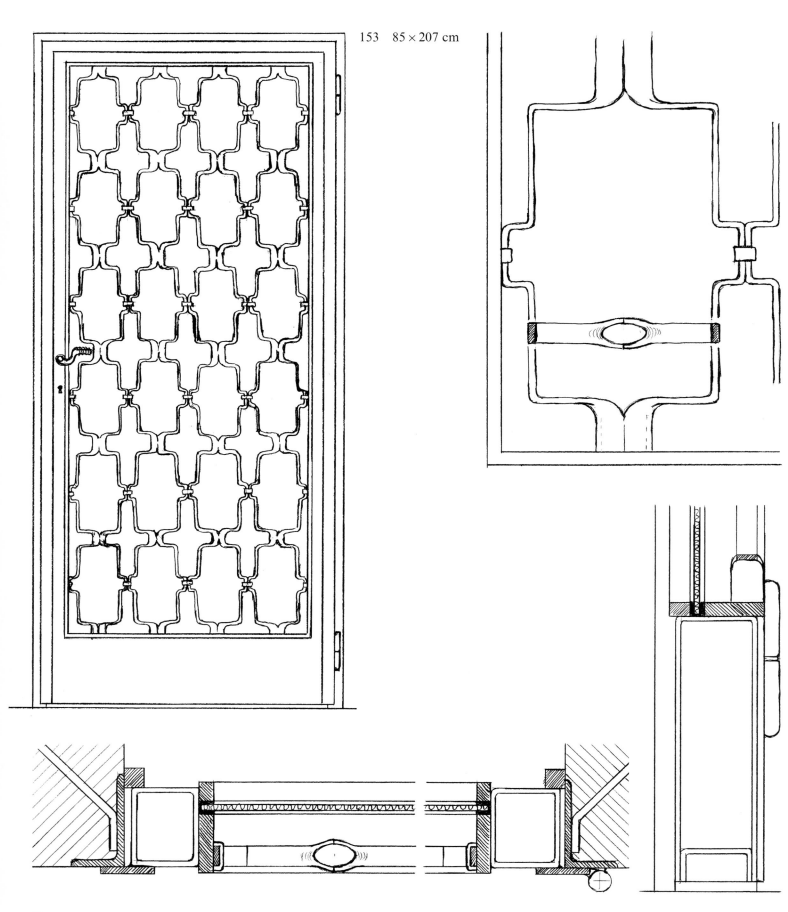

153   85 × 207 cm

154

Laternen

Kunstgeschmiedete Laternen sind in mannigfacher Gestaltung fast zu allen Zeiten verwendet worden. Hier liegt für den Kunstschmied, abgesehen von der reinen Funktion, ein schier unbegrenztes Feld an Lösungen: an der Wand, am Torpfeiler, als Sockellaterne, als Wegleuchte in Form eines Kandelabers; im wahrsten Sinne des Wortes hilft die Laterne, das zugehörige Bauwerk ins rechte Licht zu rücken. Der Lichtträger befindet sich immer im Blickpunkt des Betrachters, er soll daher nicht allein nützlich, sondern ebenso dekorativ und formschön sein. Verschiedene Effekte werden auch mit der Verglasung der Laterne erzielt. Auf den Seiten 79–114 sind zeitgemäße Leuchten in allen möglichen Variationen abgebildet. Für alle Leuchten gelten besondere Sicherheitsvorschriften in bezug auf die elektrische Installation. Sie sollte zudem möglichst wenig sichtbar sein – am besten in vorgesehener Nut oder in einem Rohr verlegt – damit der Gesamteindruck nicht beeinträchtigt wird.

Abb. 166 und 167. Diese hängende Laterne ist im Stil dem alten Laubengang angeglichen, den sie beleuchtet.

Abb. 174. Hier stammt der Baubestand aus dem Jahre 1564. Es mußte ein Kompromiß zu der neuzeitlichen Lichtquelle geschaffen werden.

Abb. 173, 189. Stillaternen.

Abb. 207. Diese Laternen auf den Treppenpfeilern gehören in einen Burghof; ihr Material ist Kupfer.

Abb. 236–241. Hier handelt es sich um Nostalgie-Laternen. Sie eignen sich vor allem für die Beleuchtung von Fußgängerzonen in alten Stadtvierteln. Natürlich finden sich auch für diese Zwecke überall beliebig viele moderne Leuchten als abschreckende Beispiele.

Lanterns

Finely wrought lanterns of many different designs have been used from time immemorial. Lanterns offer the wrought-iron craftsman a completely unlimited field of possibilities, apart from the purely functional solutions: on the wall, on the gate-post, on a base, as a light in the form of a candelabrum; a lantern helps to show a building in its best light, in the truest sense of the word. A lantern is always in direct view, and for that reason should not only be functional, but also decorative and attractive in design as well. Various effects can also be achieved with the glass used on the lantern. On pages 79–114, modern lights are illustrated in all possible variations. Special safety regulations concerning the electric installation apply to all lights. The wires should also be hidden as well as possible – preferably laid in a groove or tube planned for that purpose – so that the impression made by the lantern as a whole will not be affected.

Ill. 166 and 167. This hanging lantern is adapted to the style of the old pergola which it illuminates.

Ill. 174. Here the architectural structure dates from 1564. A compromise with modern light sources had to be made.

Ill. 173, 189. Lanterns conforming to a certain historical style.

Ill. 207. These copper lanterns on the stairway posts belong in a castle courtyard.

Ill. 236–41. Here we have lanterns in a nostalgic style, which are especially suited for the byways of a city. Of course, innumerable modern lanterns are also available.

Lanternes

Presque de tous temps on a utilisé des lanternes en fer forgé. Mise à part la fonction de l'objet, une quantité presque illimitée de solutions s'offre au ferronnier d'art: au mur, au portail, en lampadaires, en réverbères ou en candélabres. La lanterne contribue effectivement à mettre en valeur le bâtiment auquel elle appartient. Elle se trouve toujours dans notre champ visuel, c'est pourquoi elle a un but non seulement utilitaire mais également décoratif. La vitrification de la lanterne permet aussi d'obtenir différents effets.

Les pages 79–114 montrent de nombreux exemplaires de lanternes modernes.

Pour toutes les lanternes il existe des mesures de sécurité concernant l'installation électrique. Celle-ci devrait être aussi peu visible que possible – dans la rainure prévue à cet effet ou dans un tuyau – afin de ne pas nuire à l'impression globale.

Fig. 166 et 167: cette lanterne suspendue est dans le style de la vieille charmille qu'elle éclaire.

Fig. 174: la construction date de l'année 1564. Il fallait trouver un compromis avec la source de lumière moderne.

Fig. 173, 189: lanternes de style

Fig. 207: ces lanternes sur piliers d'escalier appartiennent à la cour d'un château et sont en cuivre.

Fig. 236–241: lanternes de style «nostalgique»; elles conviennent particulièrement à l'éclairage des zones piétonnières dans les vieux quartiers. On y trouve également des lanternes modernes très laides.

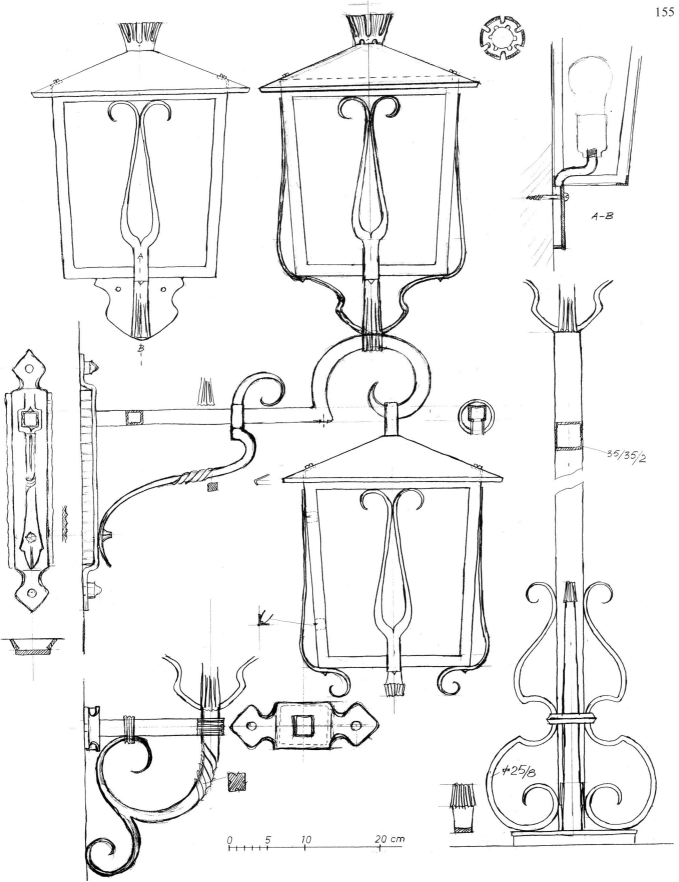

A—B

35/35/2

⌀25/8

0   5   10   20 cm

156

157

158

159

81

160, 161

162

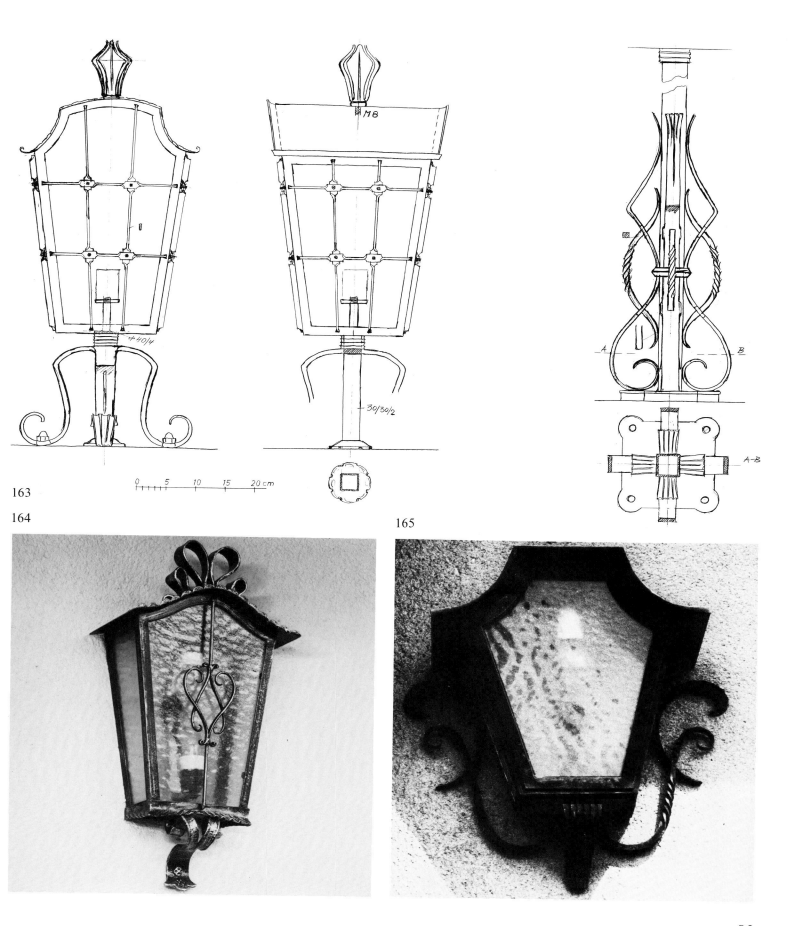

163

164

165

0　5　10　15　20 cm

83

166

167

168

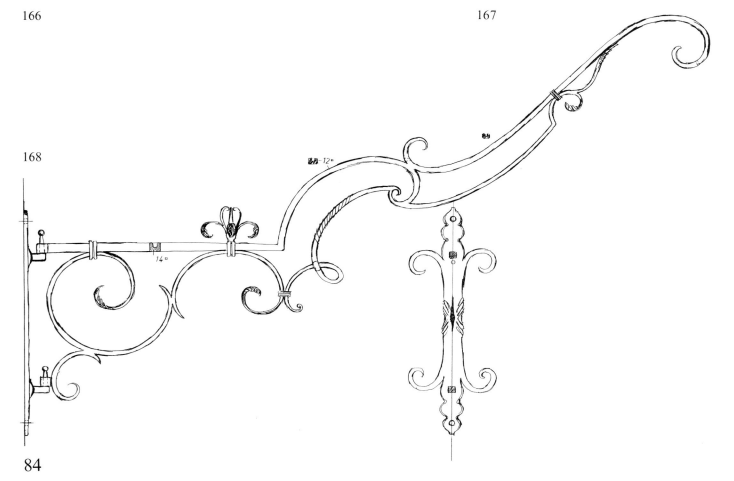

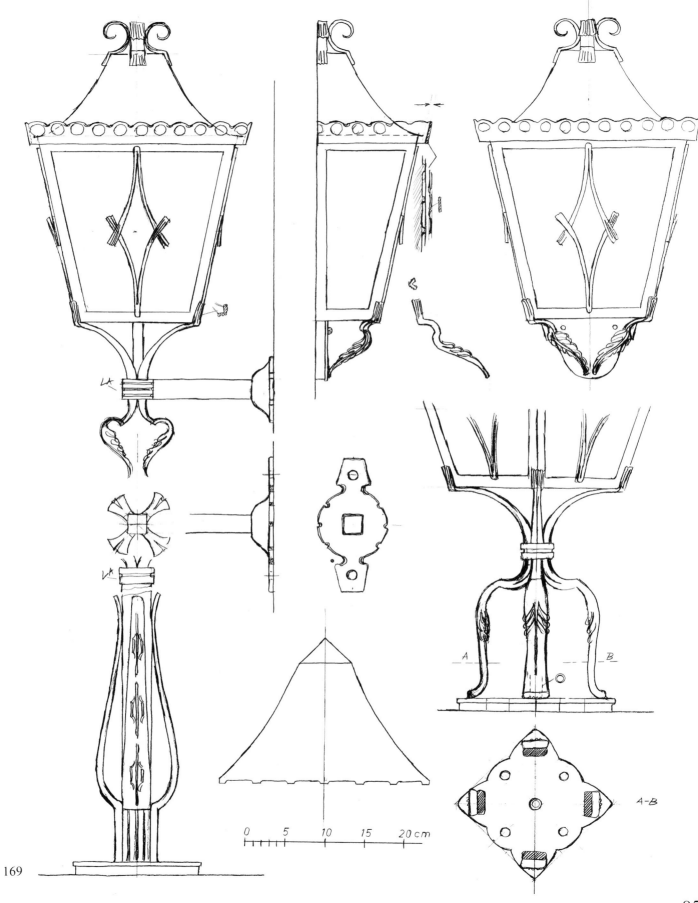

169

0   5   10   15   20 cm

A-B

173

174

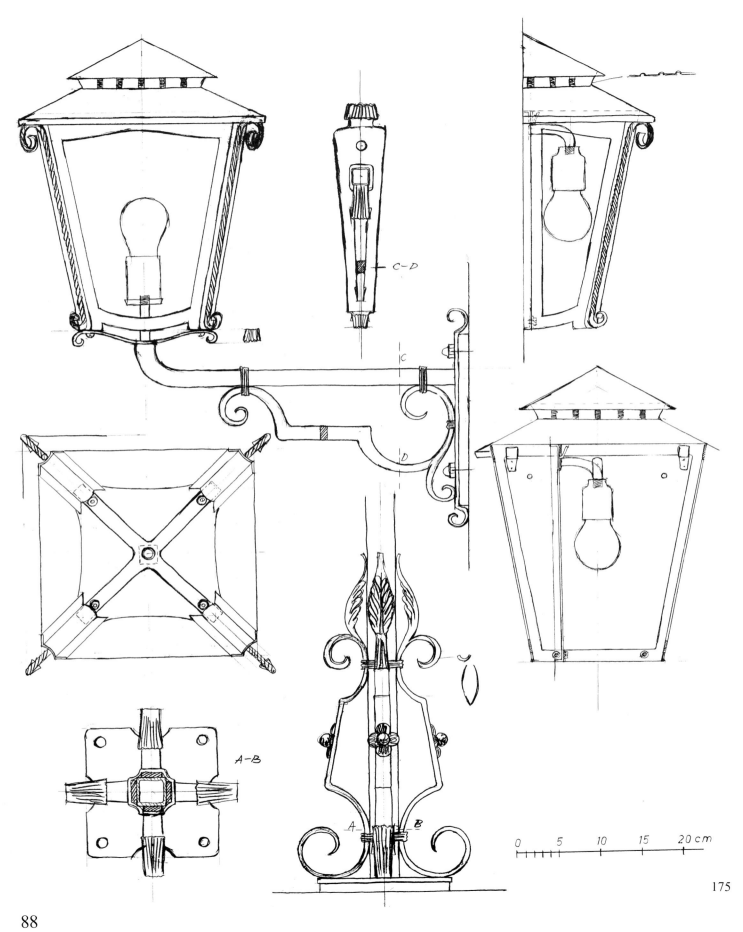

C-D

A-B

A B

0 5 10 15 20 cm

175

178

179

180

181

90

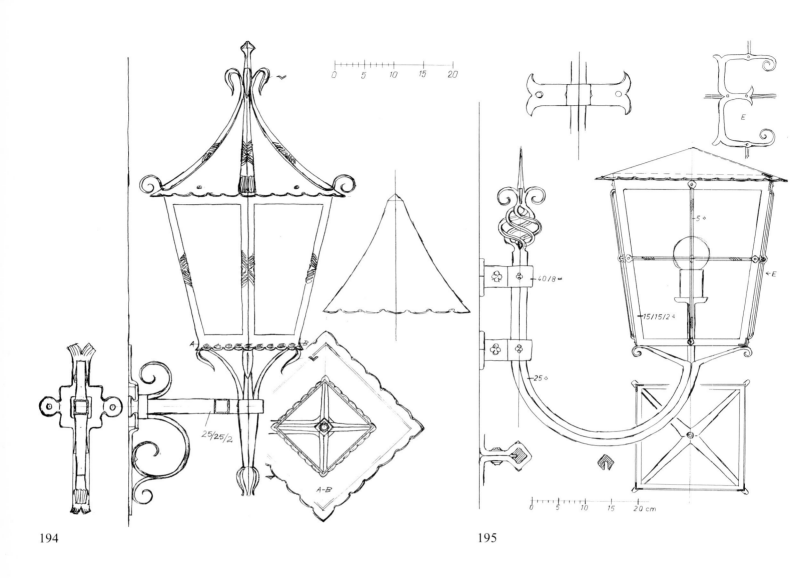

194

195

196

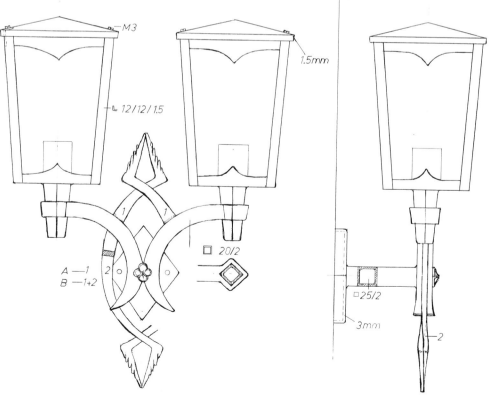

198

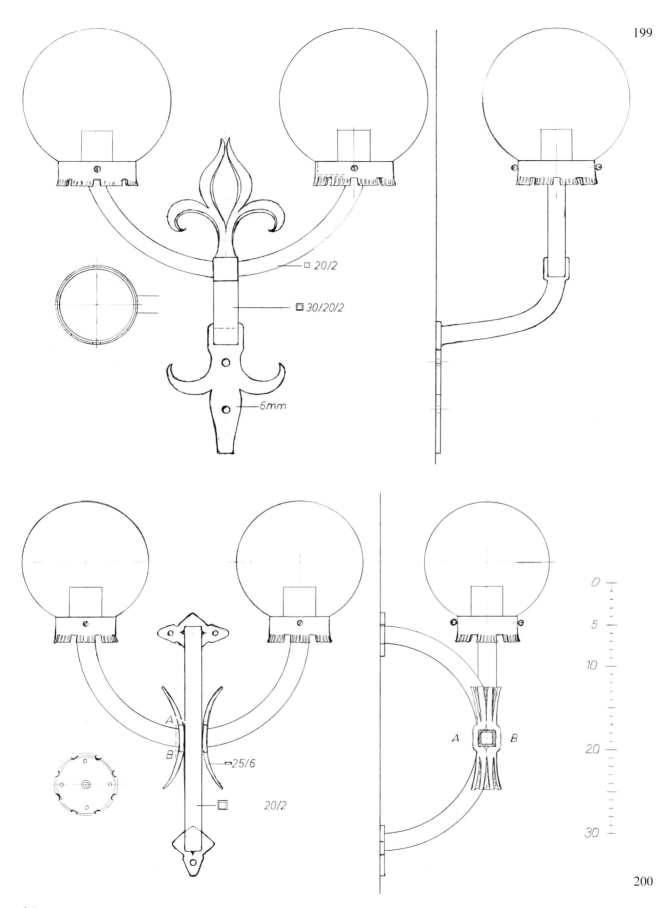

□ 20/2

▣ 30/20/2

6mm

A

B

25/6

□ 20/2

A B

0

5

10

20

30

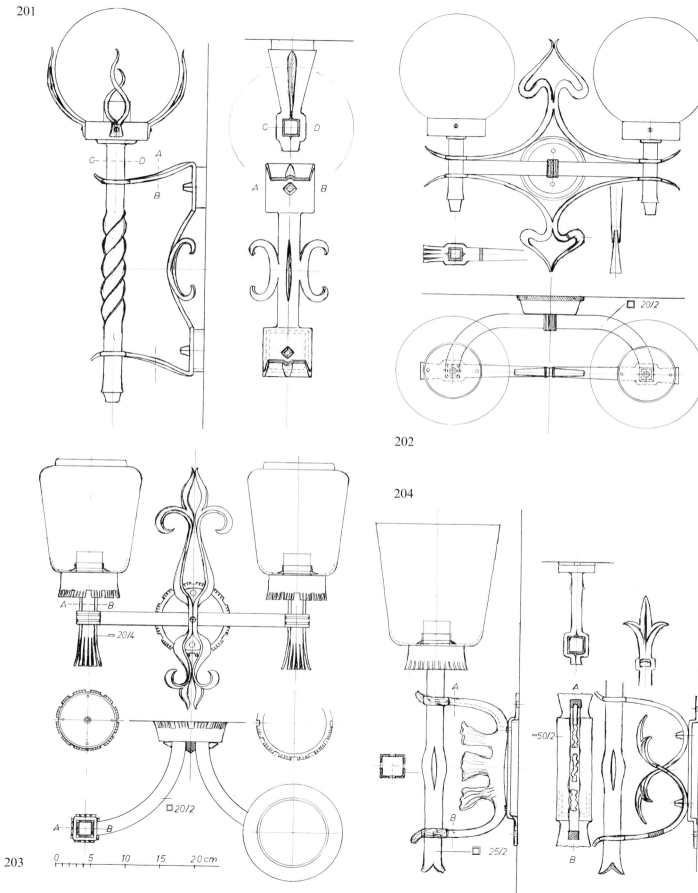

201

202

203

0   5   10   15   20 cm

□ 20/2

□ 20/4

□ 20/2

204

□ 50/2

□ 25/2

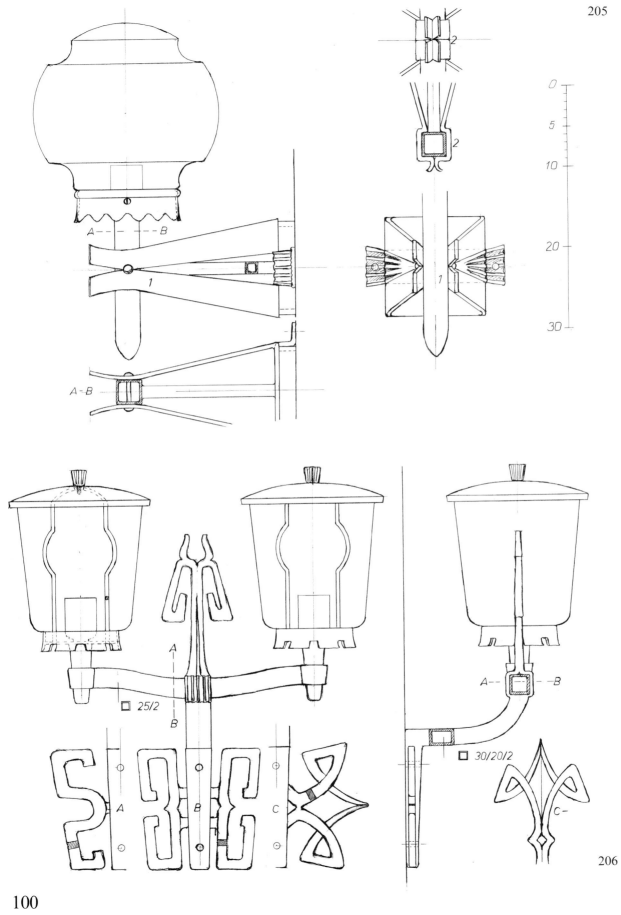

205

□ 25/2

□ 30/20/2

206

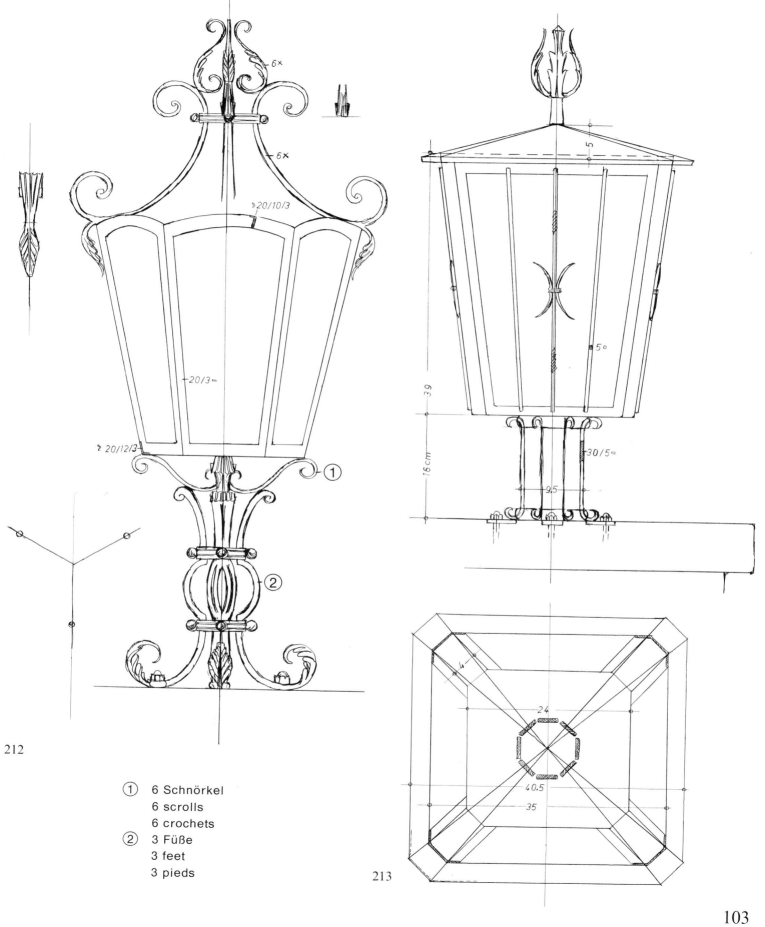

6×

6×

>20/10/3

20/3▭

⋝20/12/3

①

②

212

5

5▭

39

16 cm

30/5▭

9.5

① 6 Schnörkel
   6 scrolls
   6 crochets
② 3 Füße
   3 feet
   3 pieds

4

24

40.5

35

213

103

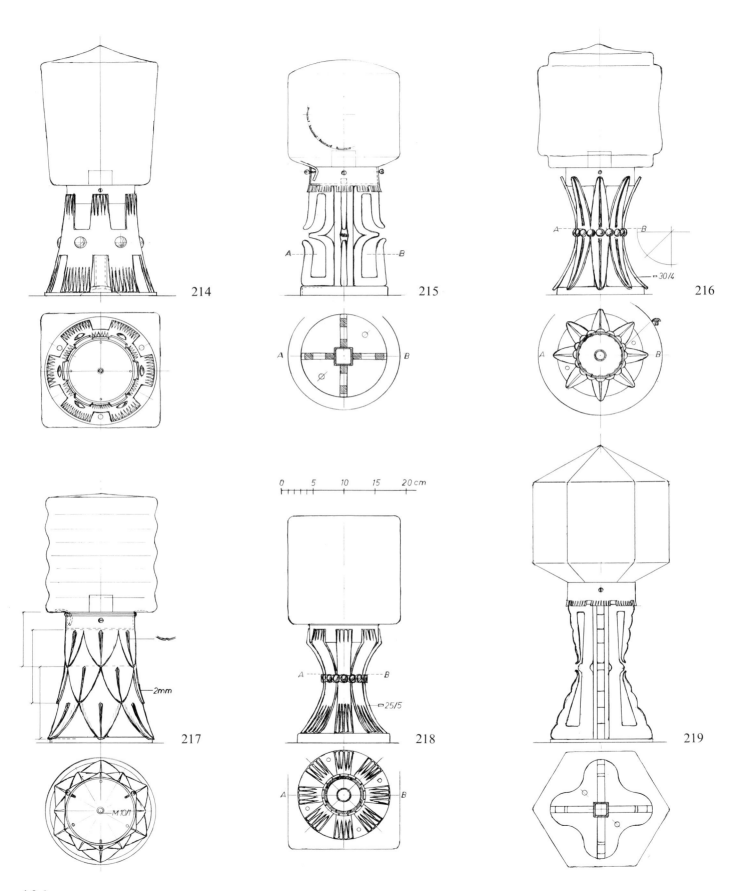

214

215

216

217

218

219

0   5   10   15   20 cm

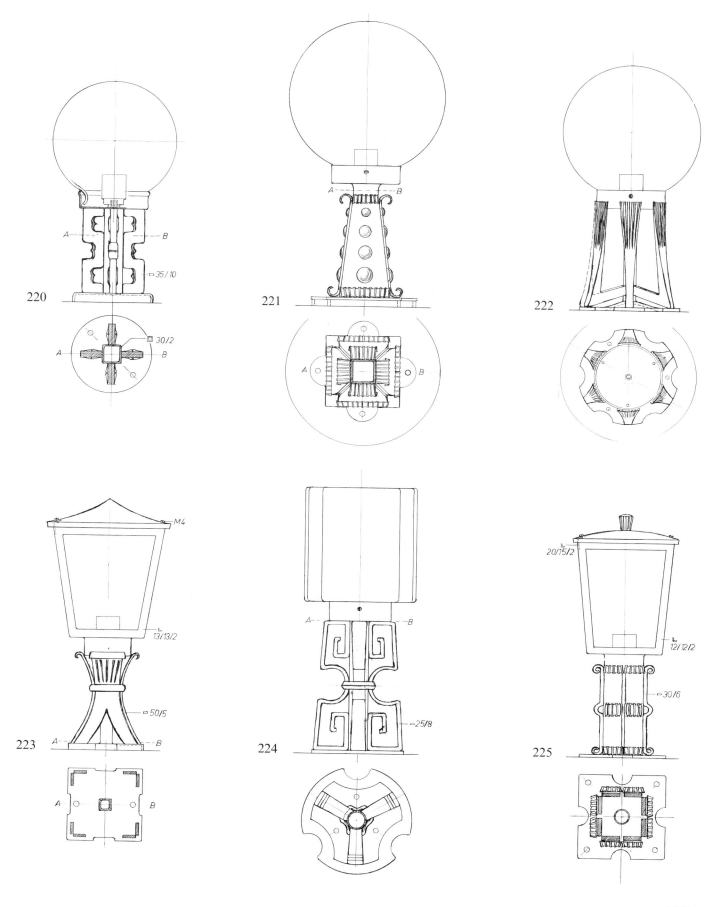

220

221

222

223

224

225

35/10

30/2

M4

13/13/2

50/5

25/8

20/15/2

12/12/2

30/6

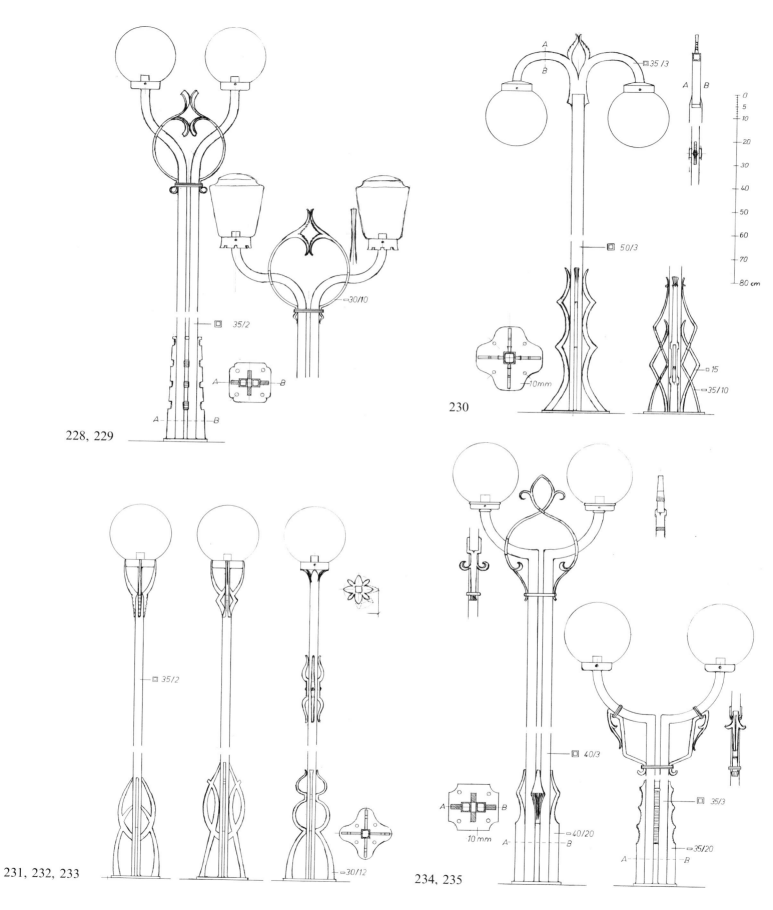

228, 229

230

231, 232, 233

234, 235

107

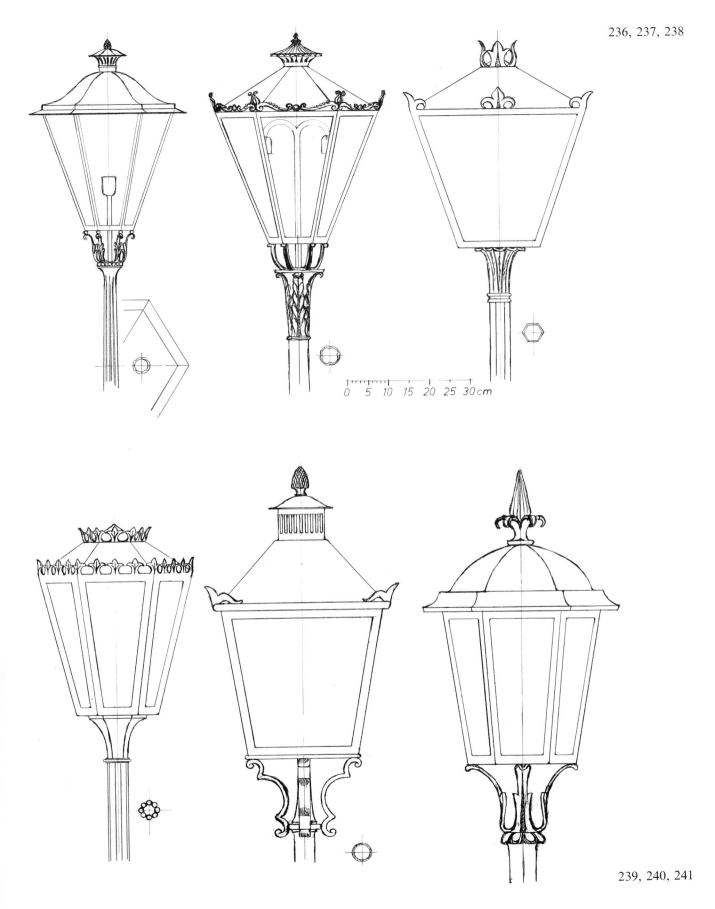

0 5 10 15 20 25 30 cm

239, 240, 241

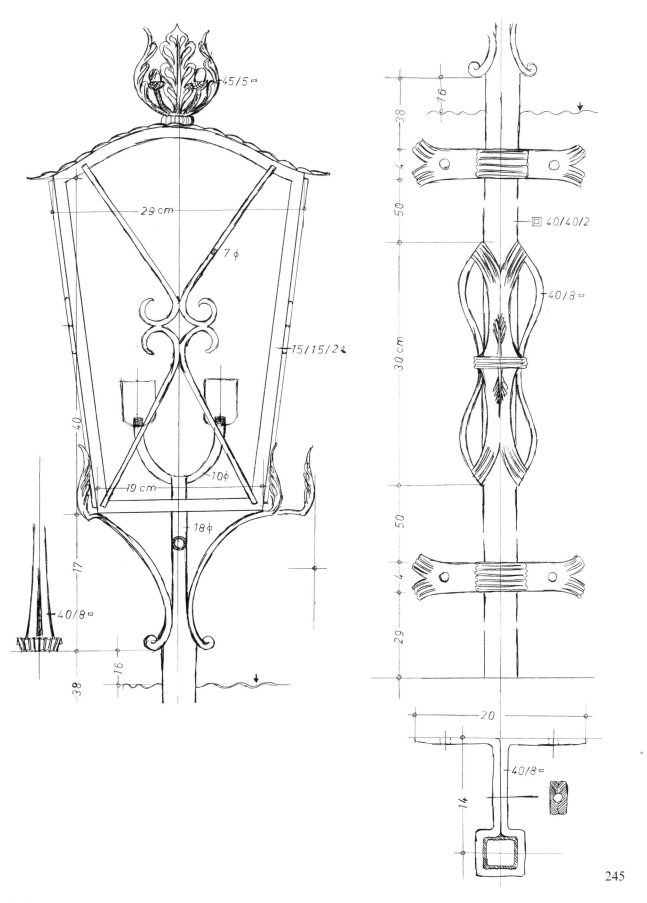

45/5▫

29 cm

7 ϕ

15/15/2↲

40

19 cm

10ϕ

18ϕ

17

40/8▫

16

38

16

38

4

50

▢ 40/40/2

40/8▫

30 cm

50

4

29

20

40/8▫

14

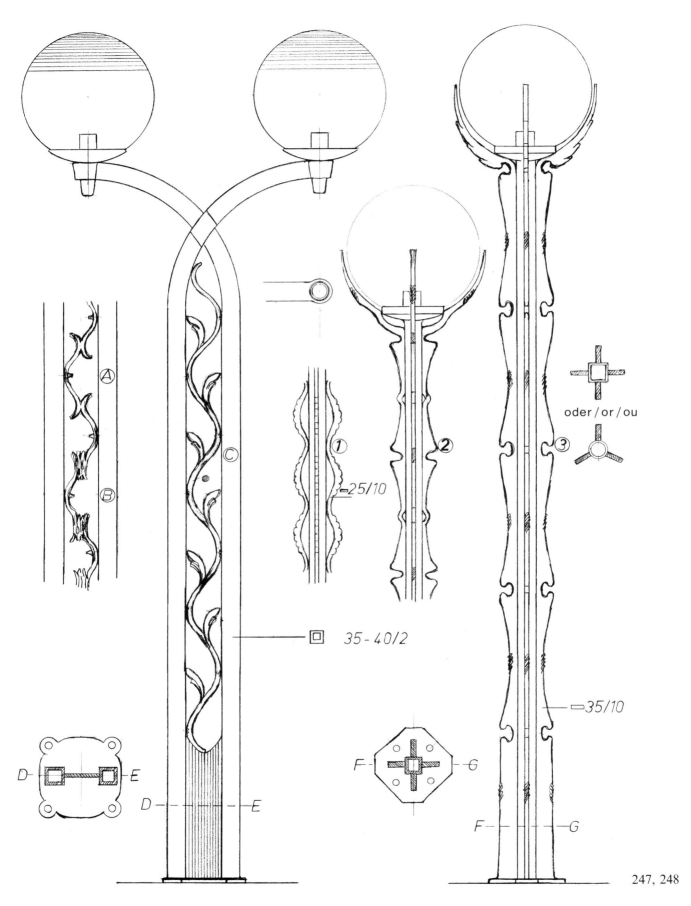

A

B

C

1

—25/10

2

▣ 35 - 40/2

3

oder / or / ou

—35/10

D   E

D — E

F —— G

F — G

247, 248

114

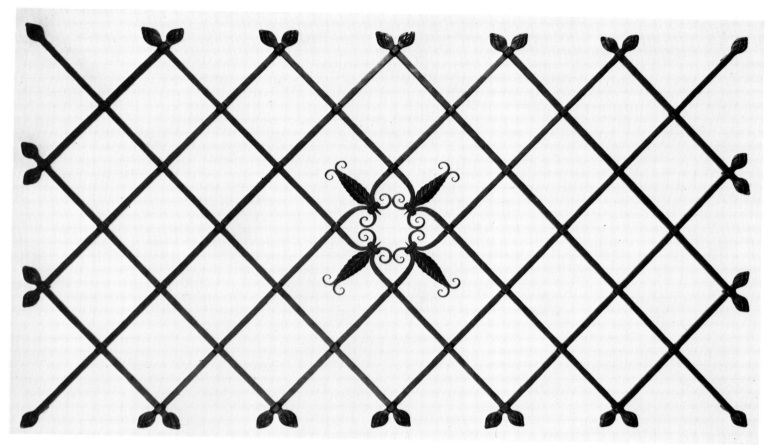

249   116 × 65 cm

Türgitter und Türoberlichtgitter

Diese Formen der Türgitter bilden nur eine Ergänzung für Holz- und Eisentüren mit Profilkonstruktion. Bei den Holztüren werden die Türgitter in allen Größen vom kleinen Durchblickfenster bis zur flächenfüllenden Dekoration gefertigt. Dabei kann das Türgitter sowohl vorstehend gearbeitet sein als auch im Holz oder im Eisenfalz montiert werden. Wichtig aus praktischen Gründen ist es, für genügend Zwischenraum zwischen Glas und Gitter zu sorgen, weil sonst die Reinigung schwierig wird.
Abb. 256, 257, 267, 279. Hier wird deutlich, daß das Türgitter wie das Türoberlichtgitter – abgesehen von der rein dekorativen Funktion – fast immer als Schutzgitter dient.
Abb. 258, 259, 266, 270, 271. Diese Gitter sind über die Türfläche vorstehend gearbeitet.
Abb. 250, 253, 262–265, 273, 278, 279, 287–297. Türgitter, die in das Türblatt eingelassen sind, erfordern einen Rahmen.

Grilles for Doors and Transom Windows

These types of grille are only to be found with wooden and iron doors of a sectional construction. For wooden doors the ironwork is fashioned in all sizes, from small window gratings to large decorative grilles that fill the door panel. A door grille can be constructed to project from the door surface as well as to fit into the wooden or iron rabbet. For practical reasons, it is important to leave enough room between glass and grille; otherwise cleaning is difficult.
Ill. 256, 257, 267, 279. Here it is obvious that the ironwork on the door and transom window – excepting the purely decorative function – almost always serves as a protective grille.
Ill. 258, 259, 266, 270, 271. These grilles are designed to stand out from the surface of the door.
Ill. 250, 253, 262–5, 273, 278, 279, 287–297. Door grilles that are set into the door panel require a frame.

Grilles de portes et grilles d'impostes

Ces formes de grilles de portes complètent seulement les portes en bois ou en fer à relief. Pour les portes en bois, les grilles sont fabriquées de toutes les tailles, depuis la plus petite lucarne jusqu'à la décoration recouvrant la surface entière. La grille peut alors être saillante ou montée dans le bois ou les rainures du fer. Il est important – pour des raisons pratiques – de laisser assez d'espace entre le verre et la grille, afin de permettre le nettoyage.
Fig. 256, 257, 267, 279: ici, on remarque que la grille de la porte ainsi que la grille de l'imposte en haut de la porte servent presque toujours de protection, en plus de leur fonction purement décorative.
Fig. 250, 253, 262–265, 273, 278, 279, 287–297: les grilles qui sont encastrées dans le panneau de la porte ont besoin d'un encadrement.

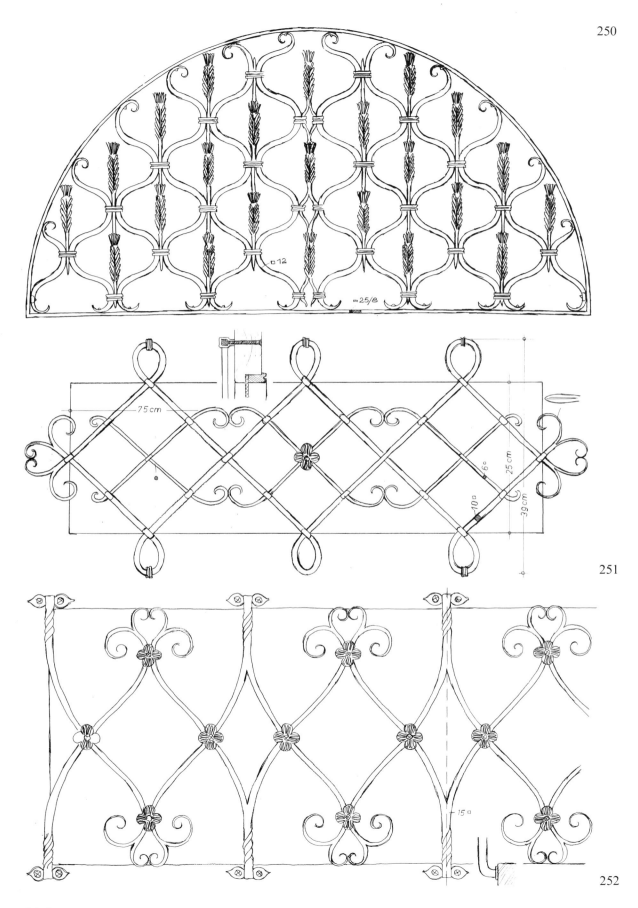

250

251

252

116

253

73 cm

66 cm

10 □

84 cm

B

A 79 cm

88 cm

12 □

M 5

256

257 72 × 144 cm

258

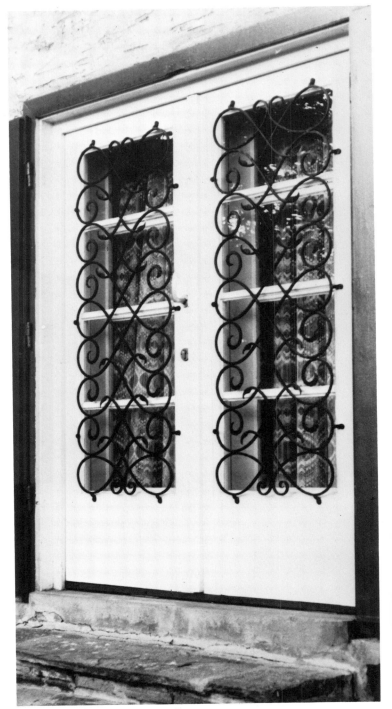

259

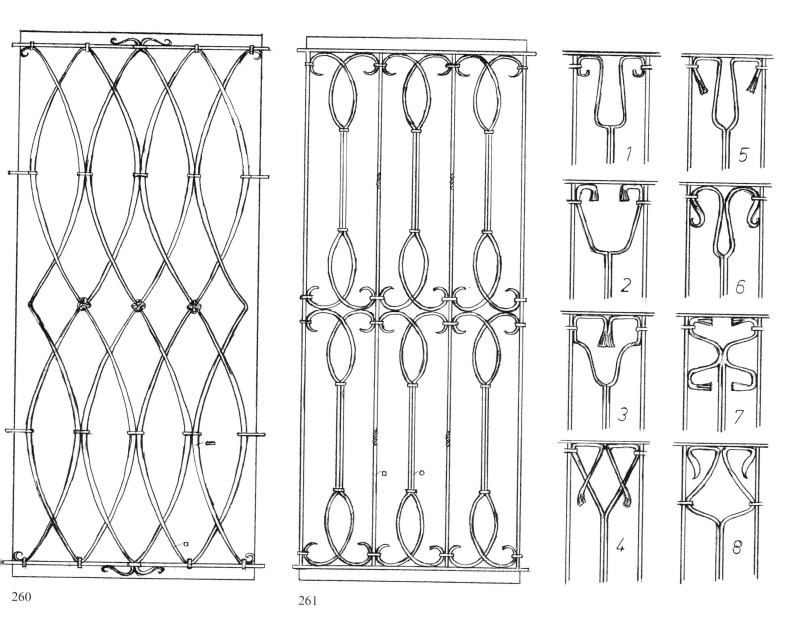

260

261

1

2

3

4

5

6

7

8

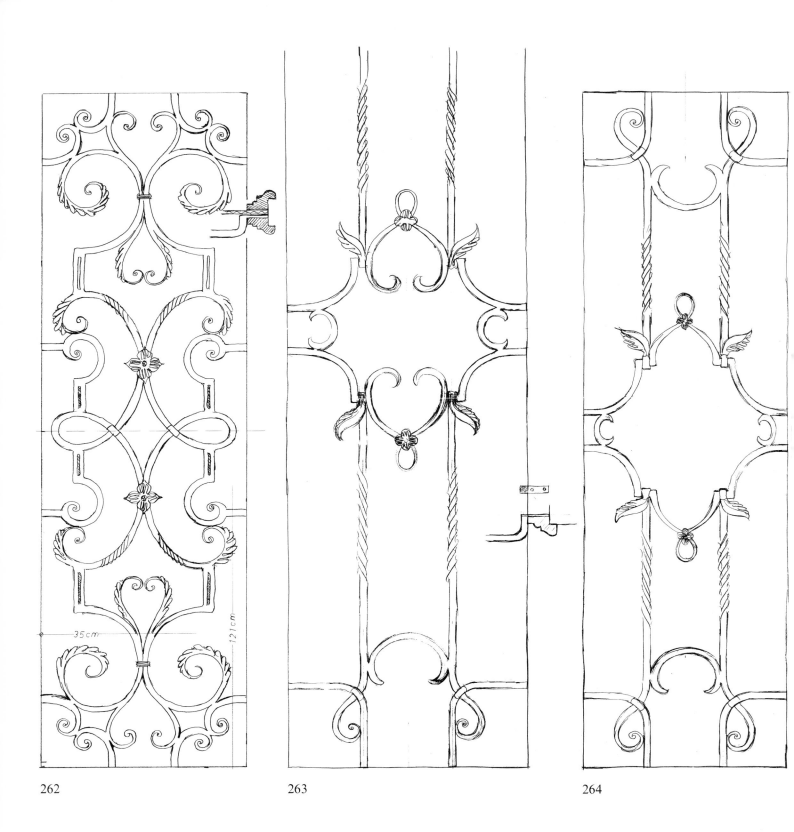

262   263   264

272

273

127

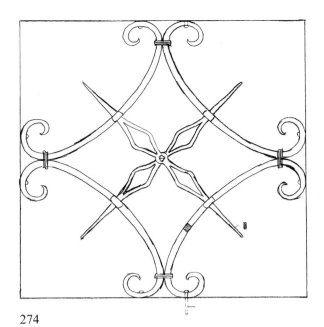

274

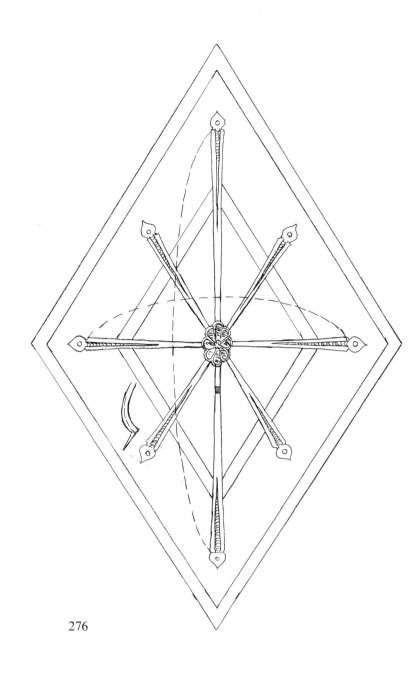

276

M 5

275

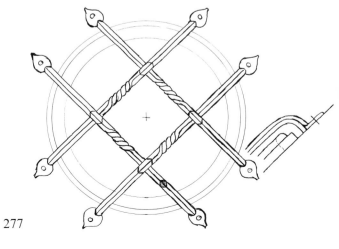

277

128

278   62 × 152 cm

279   70 × 164 cm

280, 281

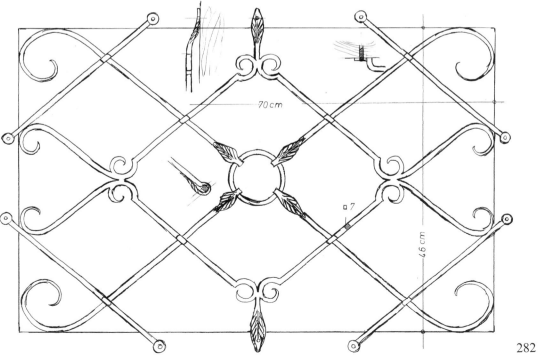

282

283   55 × 200 cm

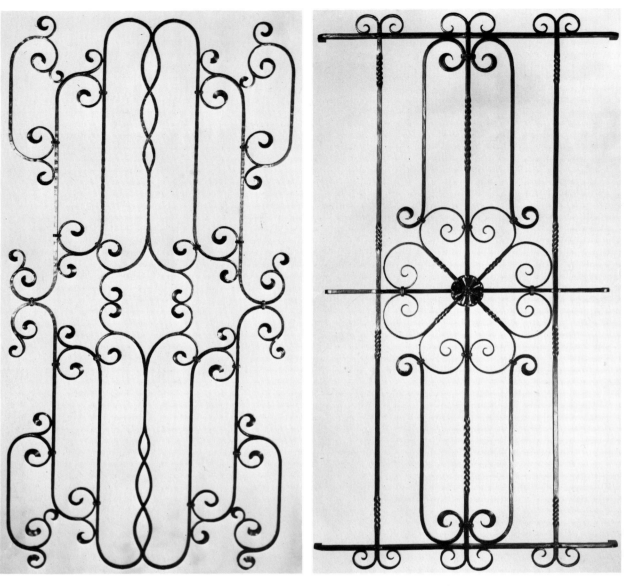

284   90 × 190 cm

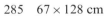

285   67 × 128 cm

286   148 × 61 cm

132

287

288

289

290

291

292

293

294

295

296

297

317

318

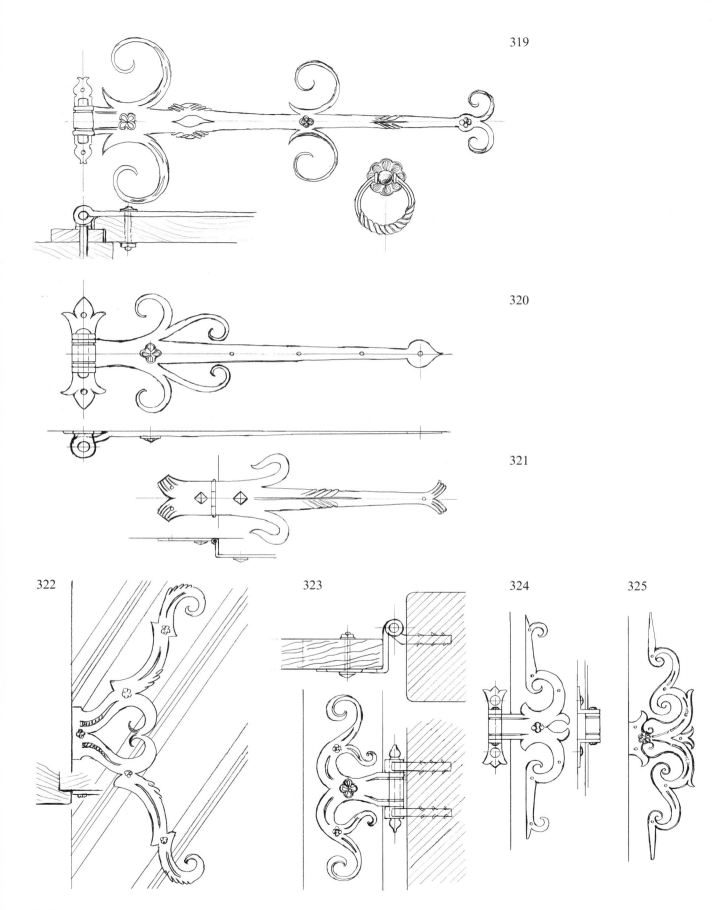

319

320

321

322 323 324 325

326

327
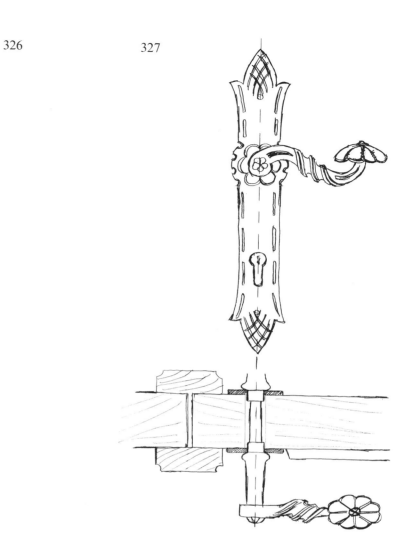

329

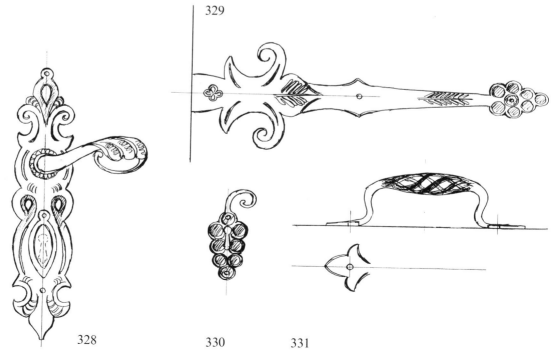

328

330

331

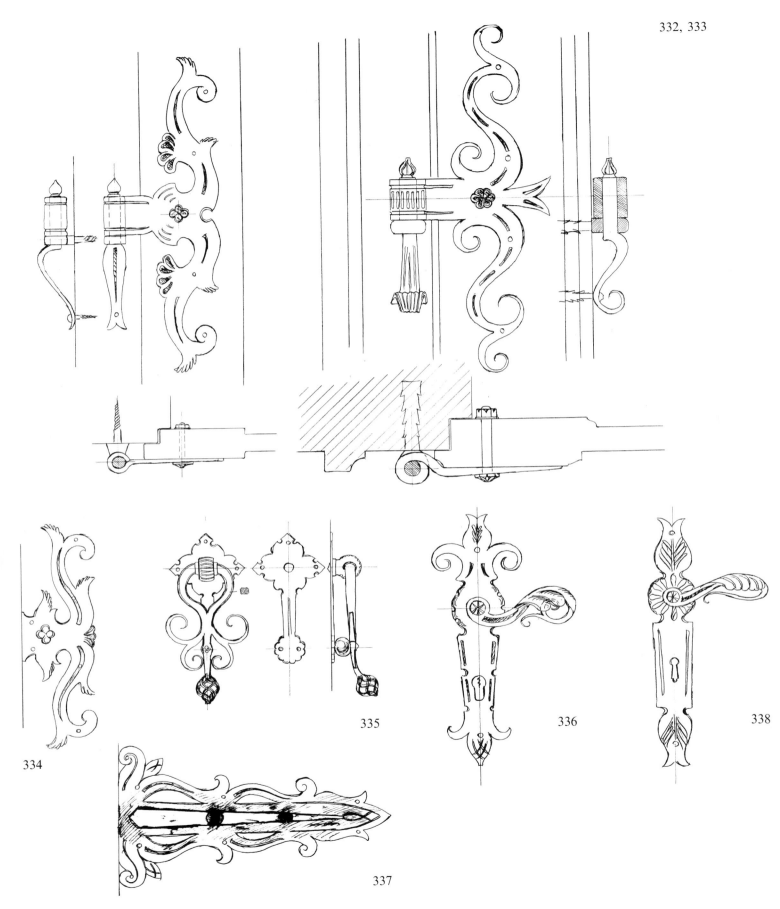

332, 333

334

335

336

338

337

142

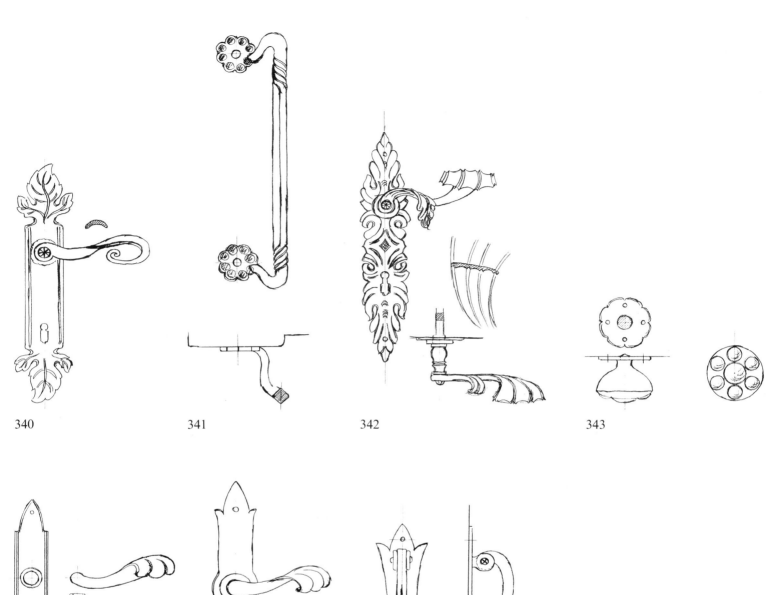

340   341   342   343

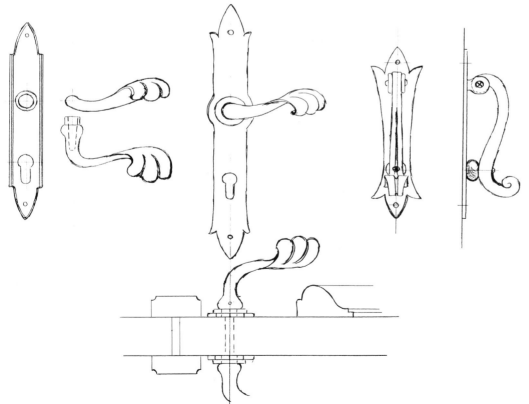

344, 345, 346

347, 348

349, 350, 351, 352

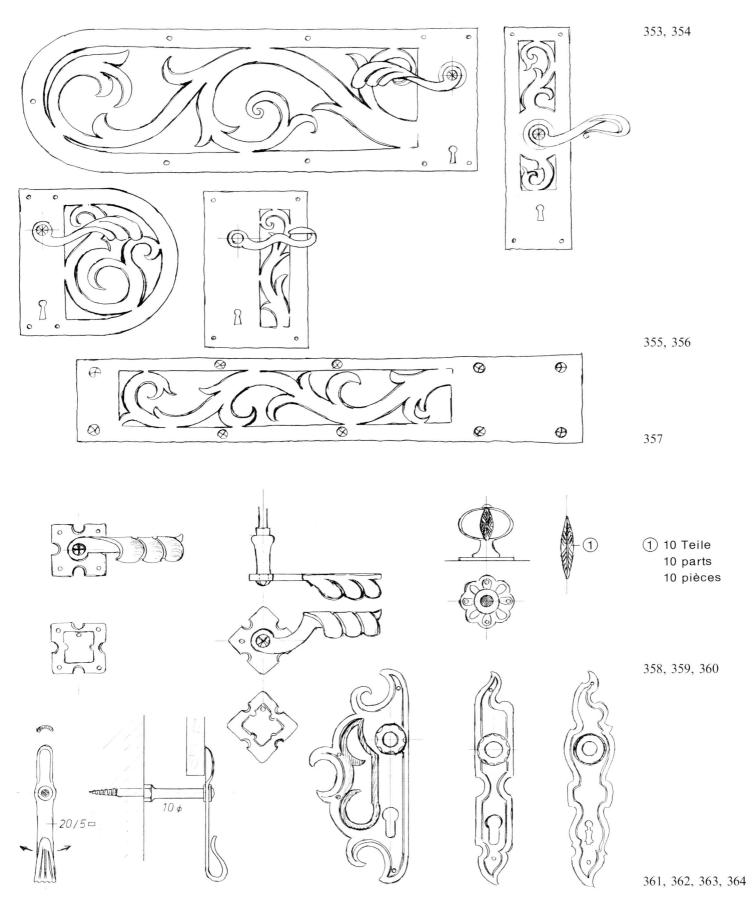

353, 354

355, 356

357

① 10 Teile
10 parts
10 pièces

358, 359, 360

361, 362, 363, 364

146

394

395

153

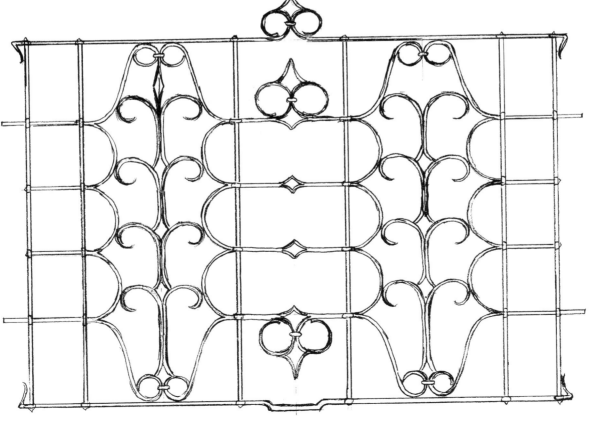

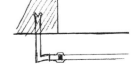

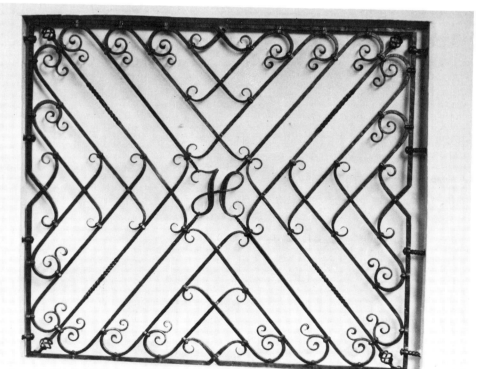

407, 408

409

410
200 × 100/143 cm

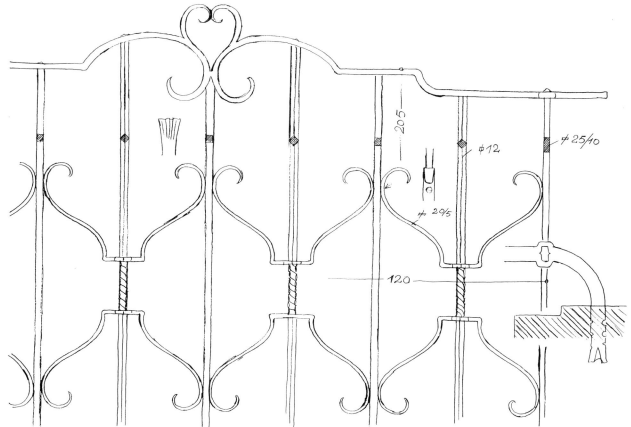

411   160 × 220 cm

412   160 × 220 cm

413   110 × 177 cm

414 98 × 106 cm

415
160 × 172/210 cm

163

417

429

430   134 × 118 cm

431   134 × 118 cm

173

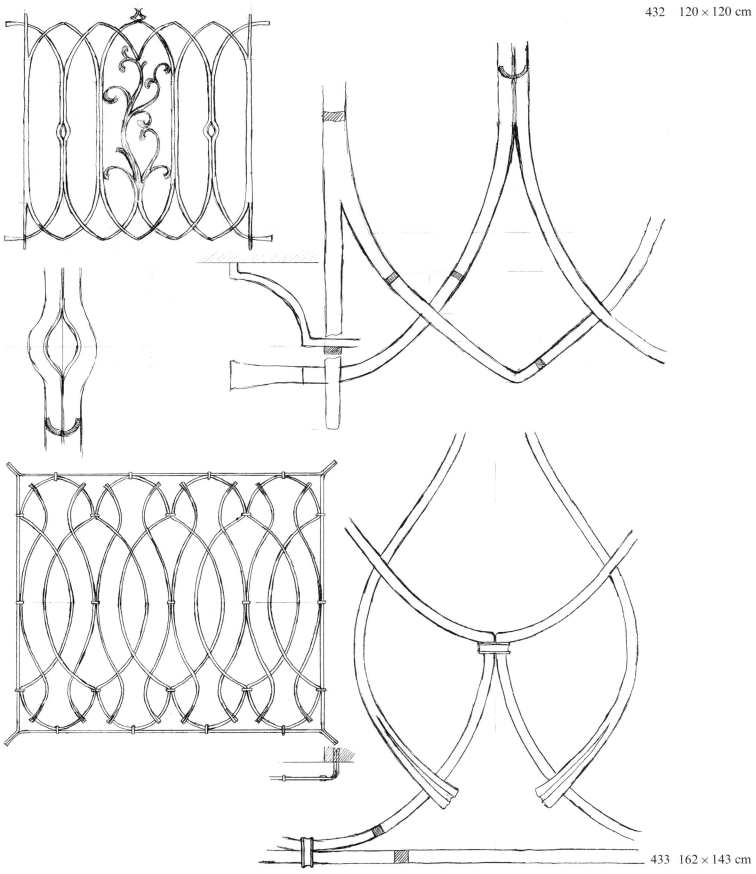

433   162 × 143 cm

174

434
182 × 200 cm

435
125 × 122 cm

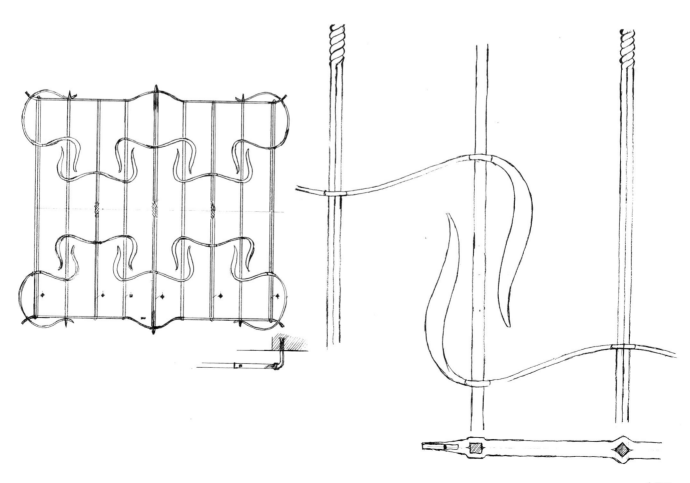

436   144 × 120 cm

437   86 × 86 cm

176

438

439

440   122 × 150 cm

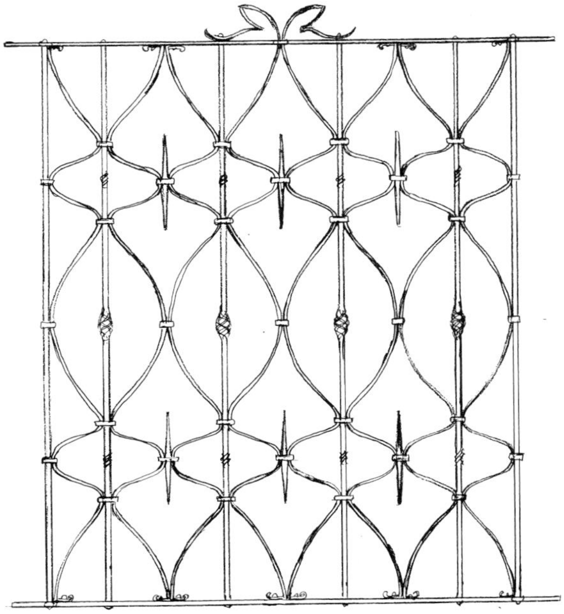

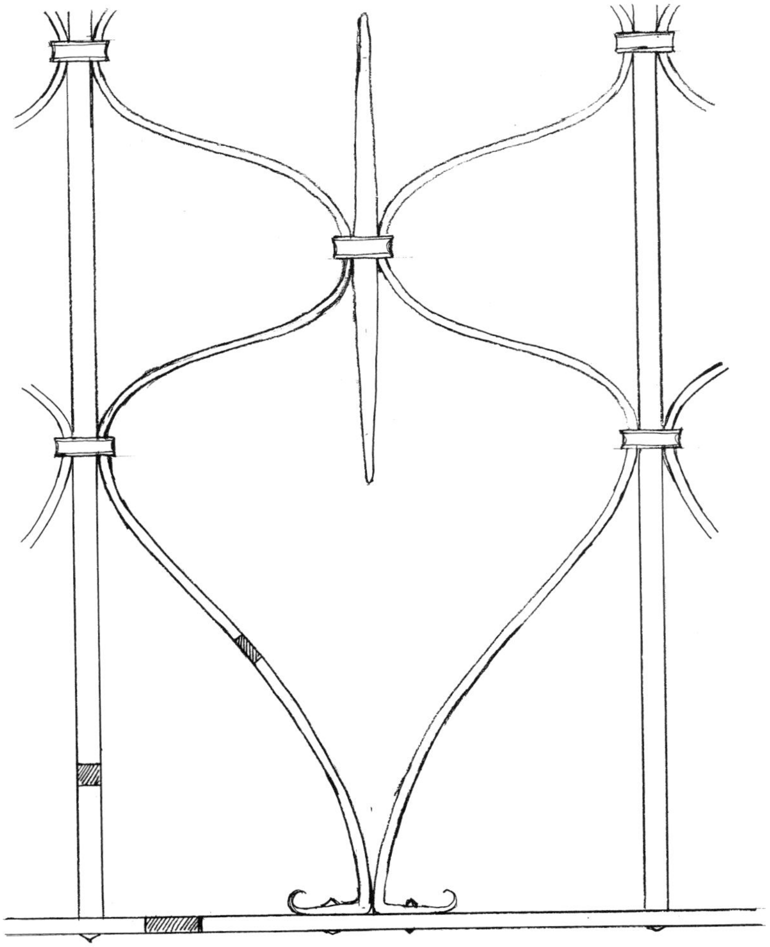

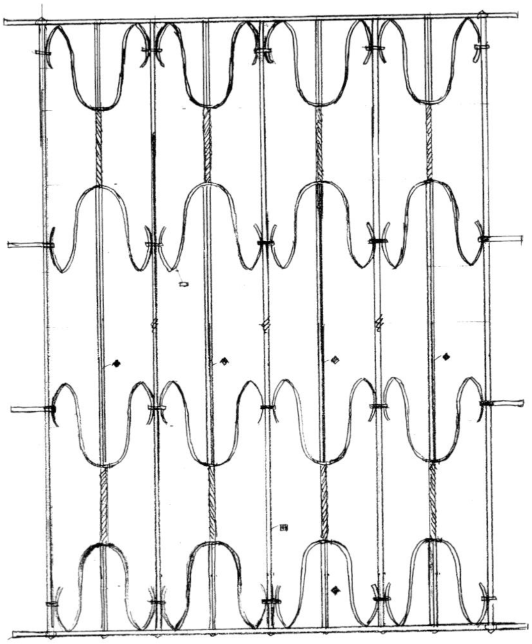

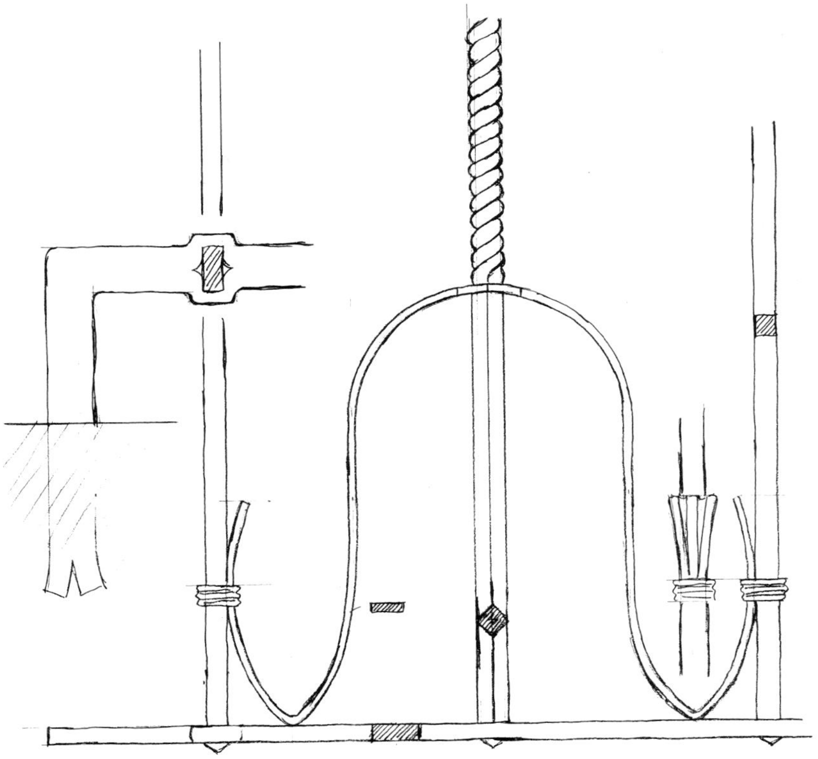

441   114 × 166 cm

178

442   176 × 120 cm

443   120 × 112 cm

179

446   100 × 140 cm

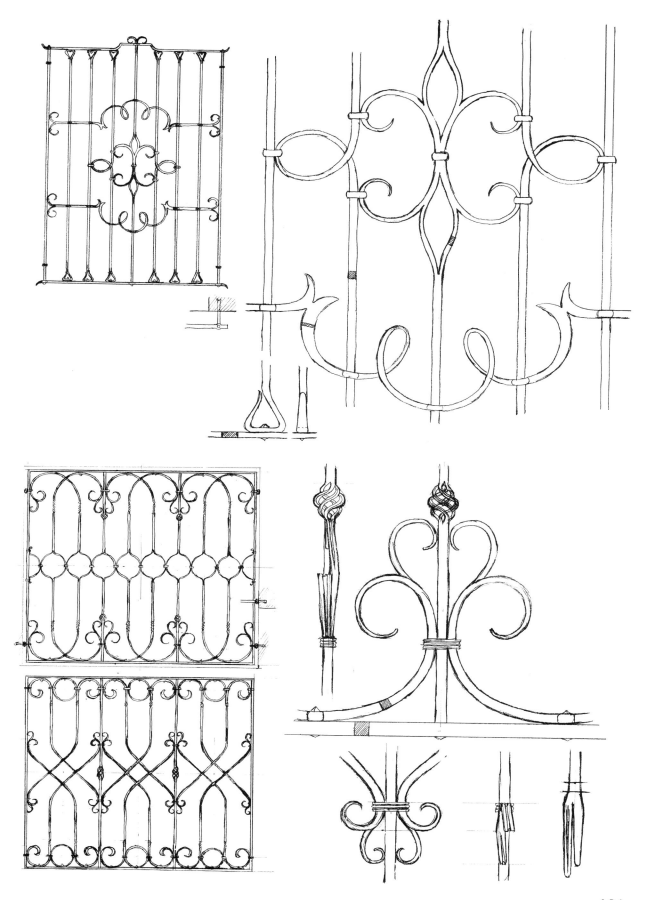

447   130 × 115 cm

181

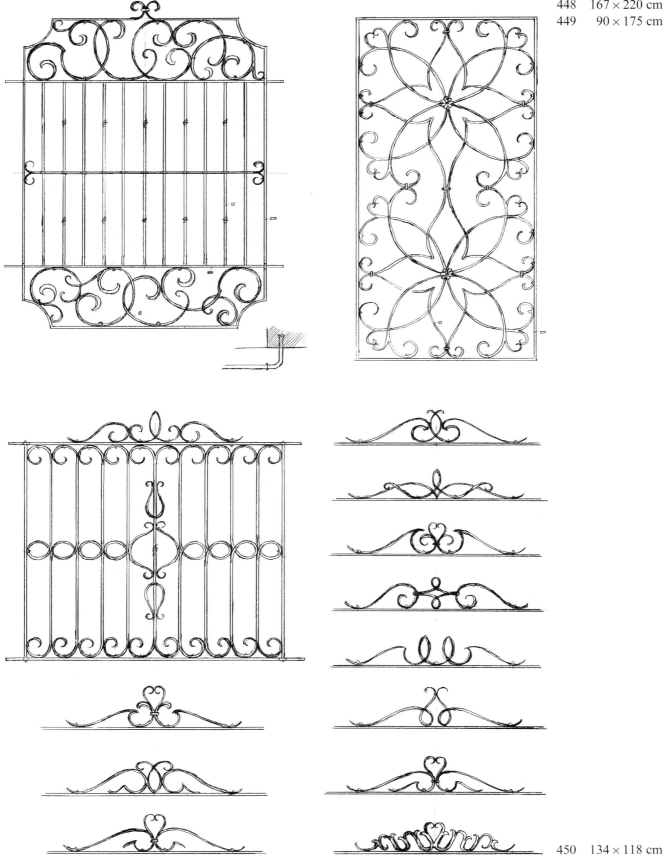

448   167 × 220 cm
449   90 × 175 cm

450   134 × 118 cm

182

451

452   70 × 70 cm

453

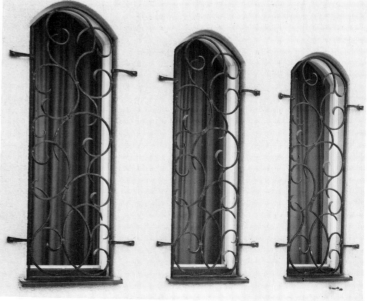

183

456

457　142 × 182 cm

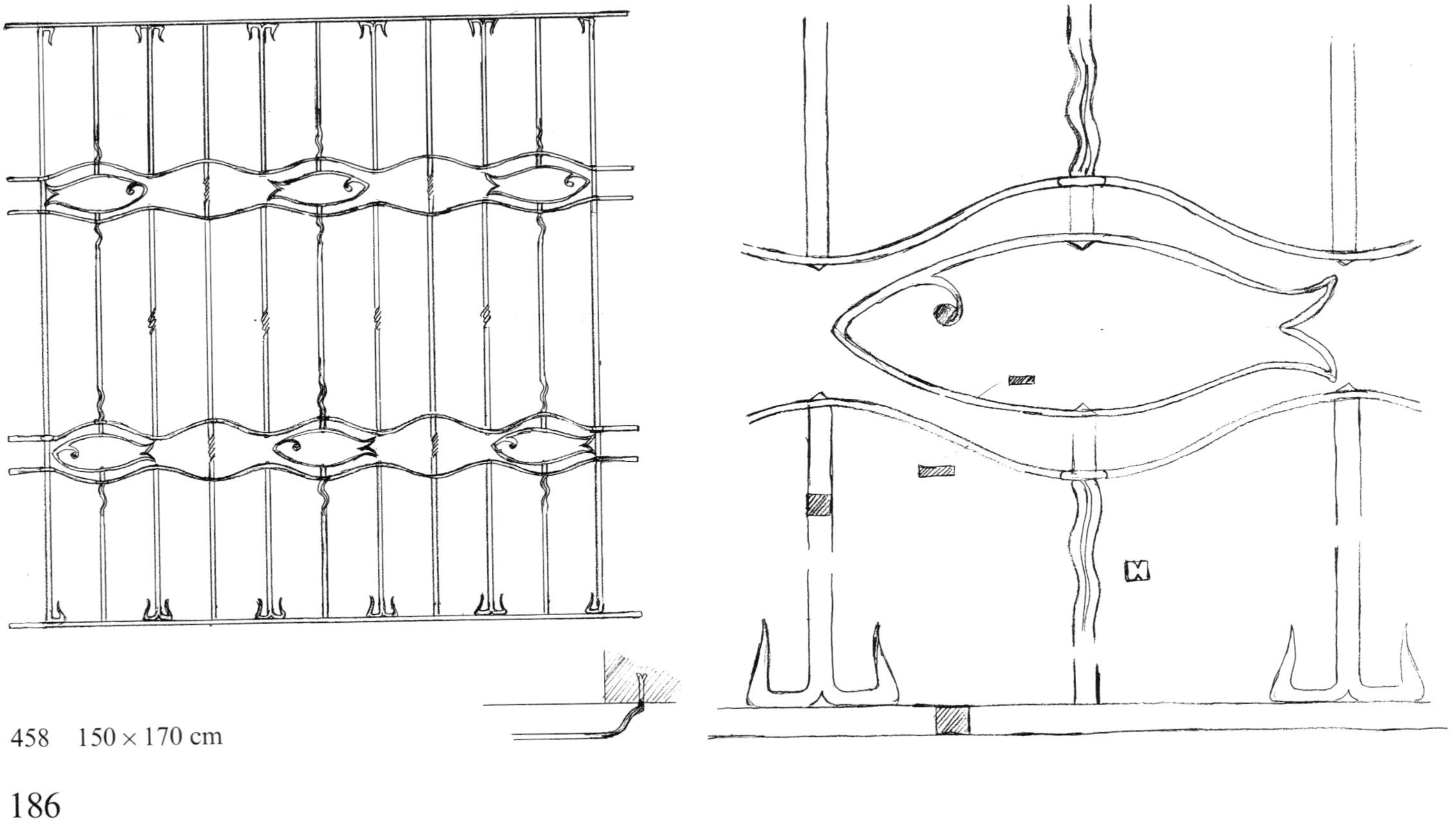

458　150 × 170 cm

459   115 × 155 cm

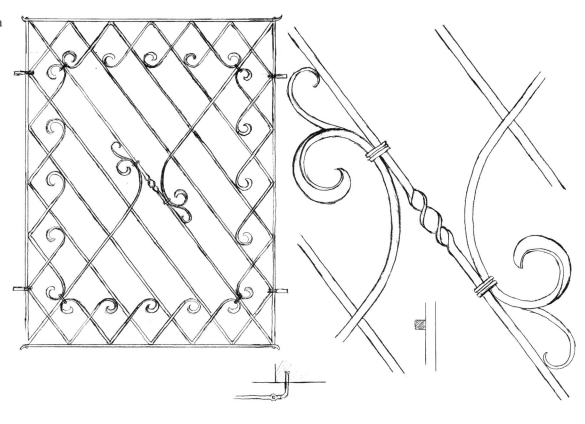

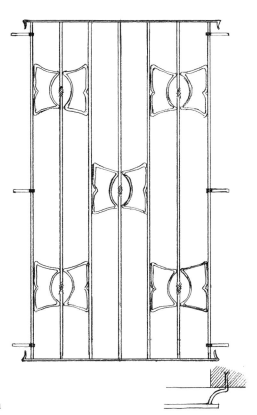

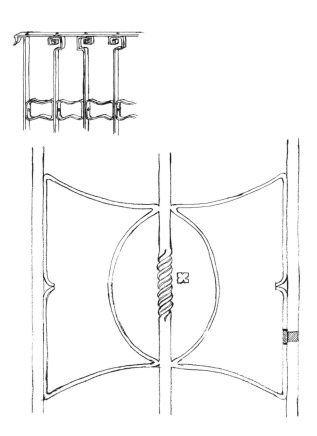

460   84 × 165 cm

462

463

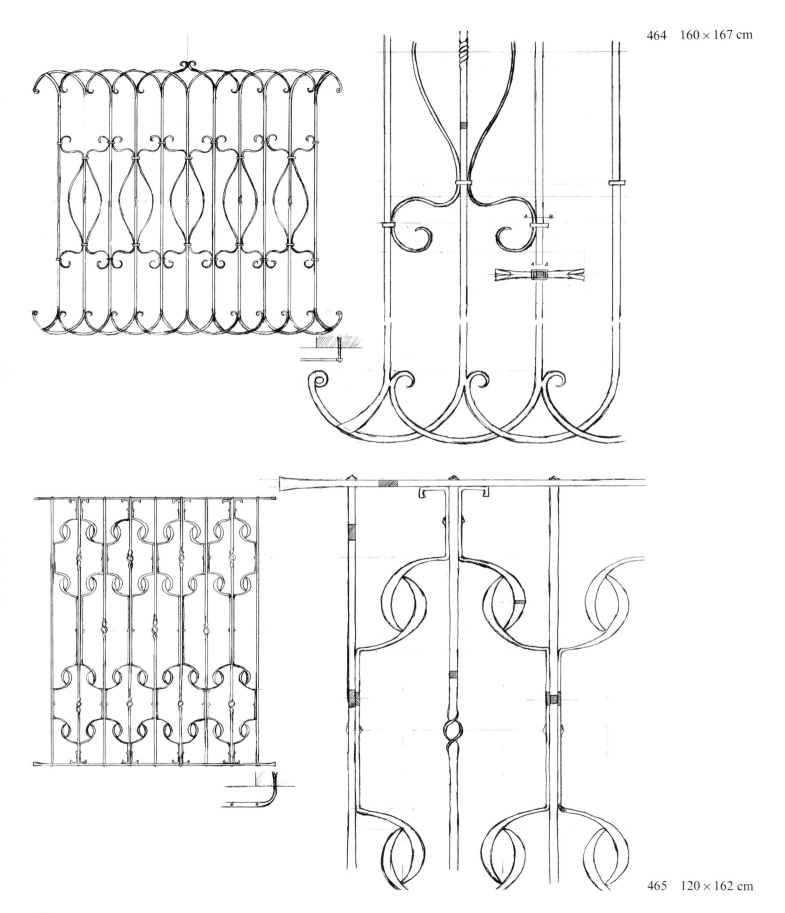

464   160 × 167 cm

465   120 × 162 cm

466

467

468

469

470

471

193

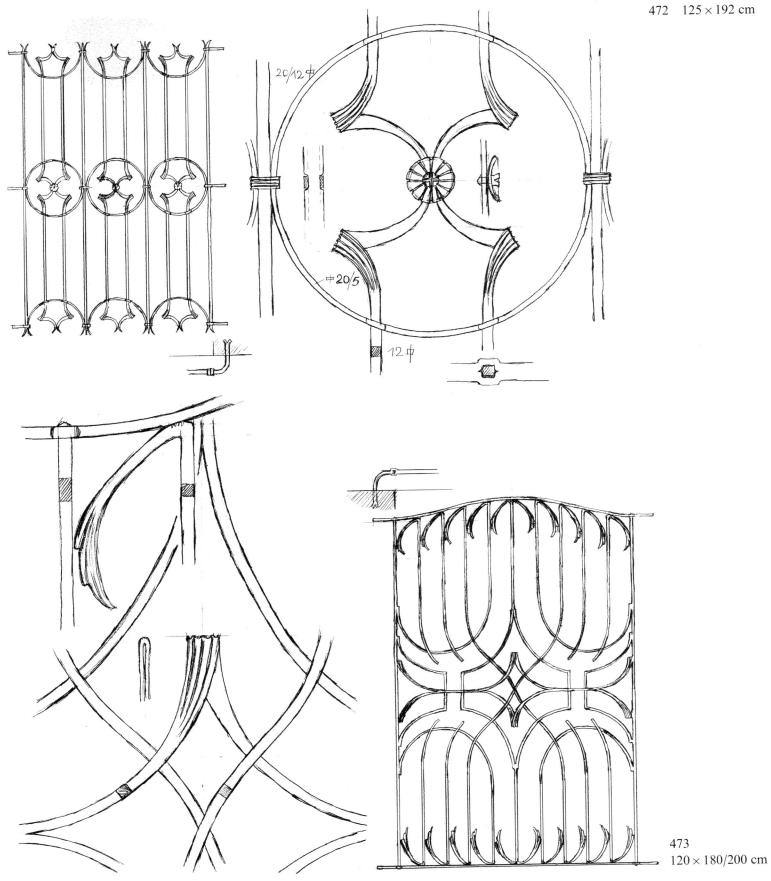

472 125 × 192 cm

20/12中

中20/5

12中

473
120 × 180/200 cm

194

474

Geländer und Geländerstäbe

Geländer unterliegen den jeweiligen Landesvorschriften in bezug auf Höhe von Stufenkante und Gehfläche bis Handlauf. Auch die Leerflächen dürfen nicht beliebig groß sein. Alle meine Werkzeichnungen und ausgeführten Geländer, wie sie auf den Abbildungen zu sehen sind, entsprechen dieser Vorschrift. Die Stababstände müssen Sicherheit bieten, dies ist bei der Ausbildung der Geländerfläche zu berücksichtigen. Die Befestigung des Geländers im Stiegen- oder Terrassenkörper ist natürlich unterschiedlich und von mehreren Faktoren abhängig.
Abb. 491. Hier wurden die einzelnen Stäbe direkt in die Stufen montiert.
Abb. 484, 495. Diese Beispiele zeigen tragende Hauptstützen in bestimmten Abständen und eine durchgehende untere Leiste in Abstand vom Fußbogen bzw. von den Stufen.
Abb. 499 und 502 zeigen besonders gut, wie die Arabesken unmittelbar am Stufenkörper befestigt sind.
Abb. 474, 509, 514. Die über die Holzwange geführten Stützen geben dem Gitter mehr Halt und unterteilen zugleich die Blende.
Abb. 516–568. Die Vielzahl der Geländerstäbe, die auf den Werkzeichnungen zu sehen sind, können beliebig aneinandergereiht, mit glatten Zwischenstäben unterbrochen oder je nach Geschmack vereinfacht ausgeführt werden. Ich habe darauf verzichtet, Eisenstärken anzugeben. Dies sei jedem selbst überlassen. Zu empfehlen ist allenfalls, dem Bauherrn ein Musterstück vorzulegen.

Balustrades and Balusters

Balustrades are often subject to State regulations regarding distance from the edge of the step and from the tread to the handrail. The open spaces are likewise limited to a certain size. All of my working drawings and completed balustrades, as can be seen in the illustrations, are done in accordance with these regulations. It must be considered in the construction of a balustrade wether the distance between balusters is a safe one. How the banister is attached to the stairway or patio varies, of course, and is dependent on many factors.
Ill. 491. Here the individual balusters were mounted directly into the steps.
Ill. 484, 495. These examples show main supports at set distances and a continuous lower rail above the floor or the steps.
Ill. 499 and 502 show particularly well how the arabesques may be fastened directly to the stairway structure.
Ill. 474, 509, 514. The rails placed over the stringboard afford the balustrade more support, and at the same time visually divide the facing.
Ill. 516–68. The various balusters which can be seen in the working drawings can be placed in any order, be alternated with flat rails, or, if one prefers, be fashioned in a simpler form. I have chosen not to give the thickness of the iron. This is left up to each craftsman to decide. In any case, I recommend showing the client a sample.

Rampes, balustrades et barreaux

La hauteur des rampes et balustrades est soumise, suivant les pays, à certaines prescriptions, les espaces vides également. Pour façonner rampes et balustrades, il faut tenir compte de l'intervalle entre les barreaux qui est un facteur de sécurité. Les rampes d'escaliers et les balustrades de terrasses sont fixées de façons différentes; et ceci dépend de plusieurs facteurs.
Fig. 491: ici les barreaux ont été fixés directement dans les marches.
Fig. 484, 495: ces exemples montrent des éléments de support placés à intervalles les uns des autres et traversés en bas par une barre, à une certaine distance des marches.
Les figures 499 et 502 montrent particulièrement bien comment les arabesques sont fixées directement aux marches.
Fig. 474, 509, 514: les supports sur le limon en bois donnent à la grille plus de stabilité et partagent en même temps le volet.
Fig. 516–568: les barreaux que l'on peut voir sur les ébauches peuvent être assemblés suivant le goût de chacun; ils peuvent être interrompus par des barreaux lisses ou encore être exécutés de façon très simple. J'ai renoncé à donner des indications quant à l'épaisseur du fer; à chacun d'en décider. Il est recommandé en tout cas de présenter un échantillon au client.

475

476

477

478

196

483

484

485

486, 487

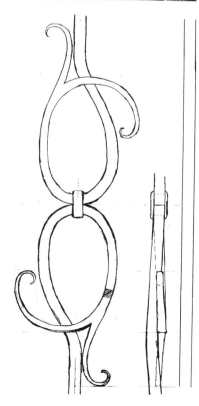

488

199

489

490

200

491

492

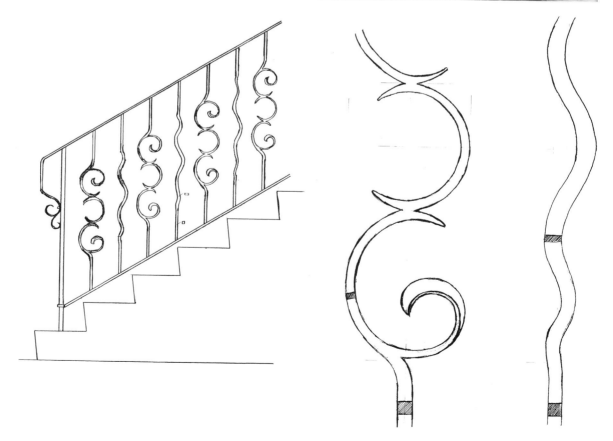

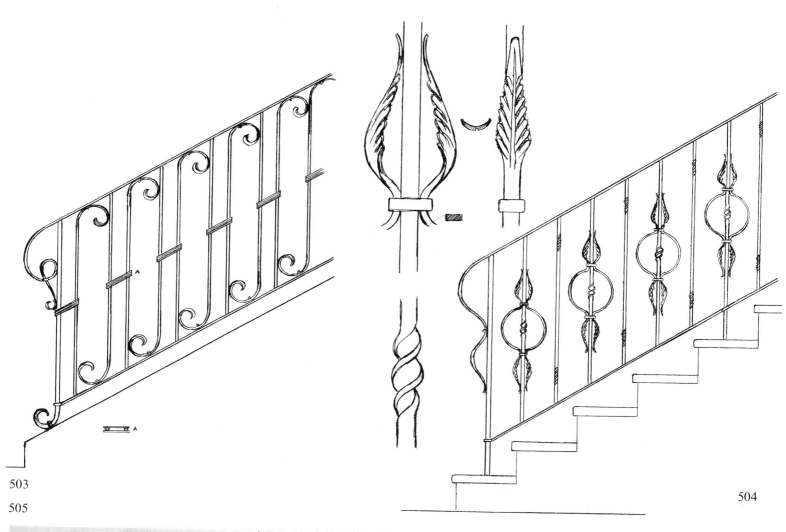

503

505

504

507

508

211

509

513, 514, 515

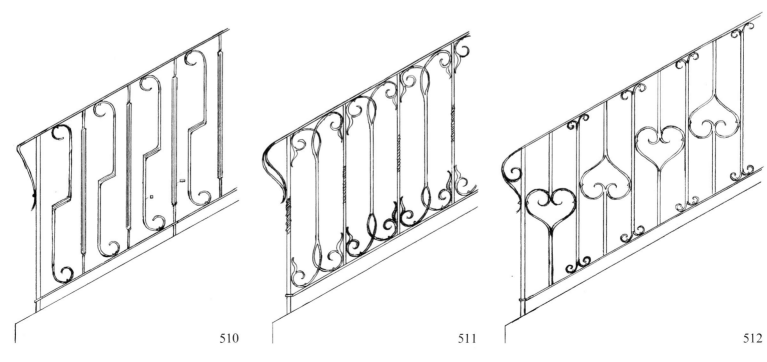

510

511

512

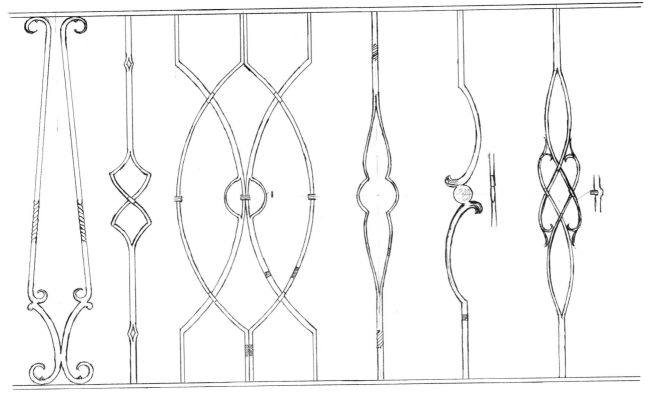

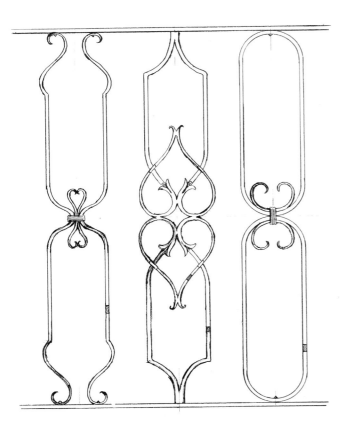

214

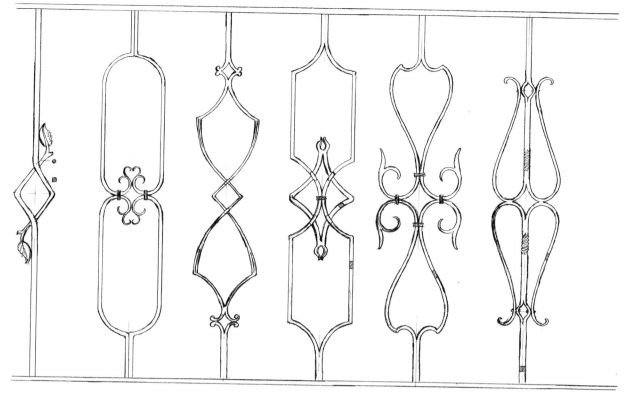

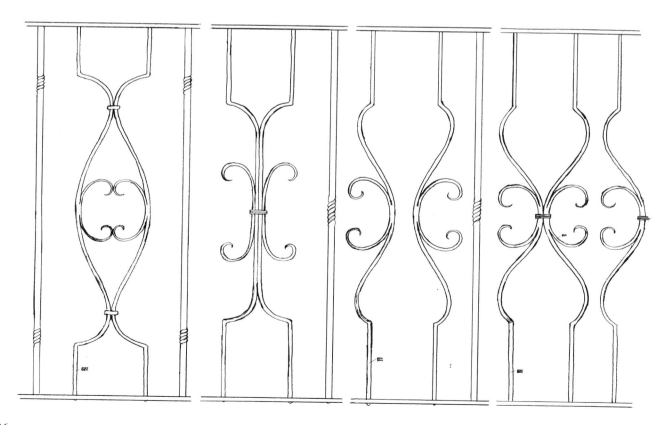

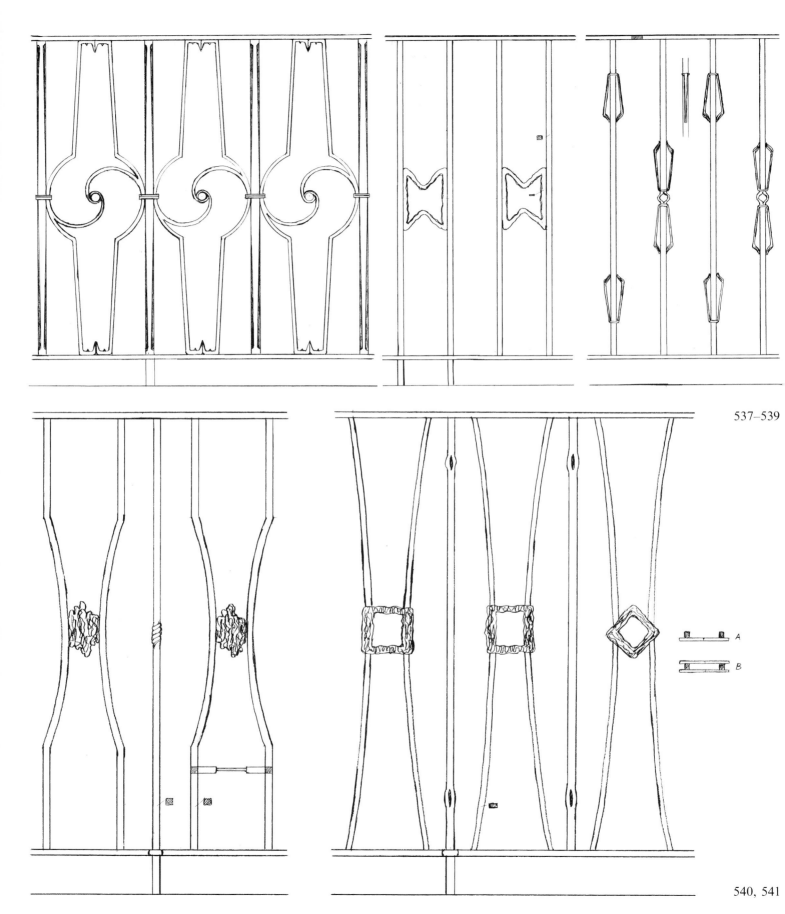

537–539

540, 541

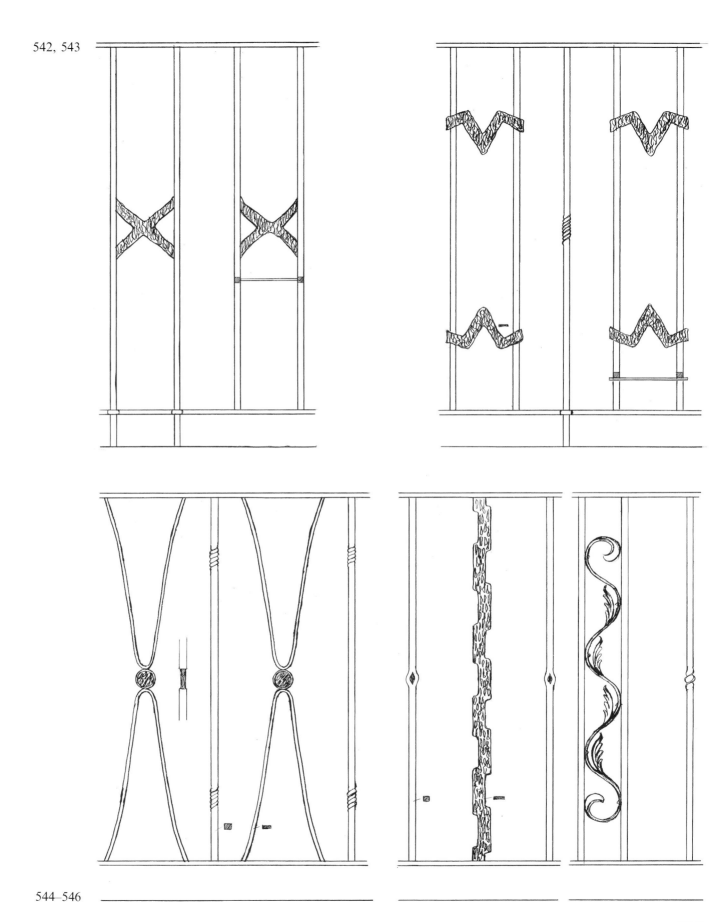

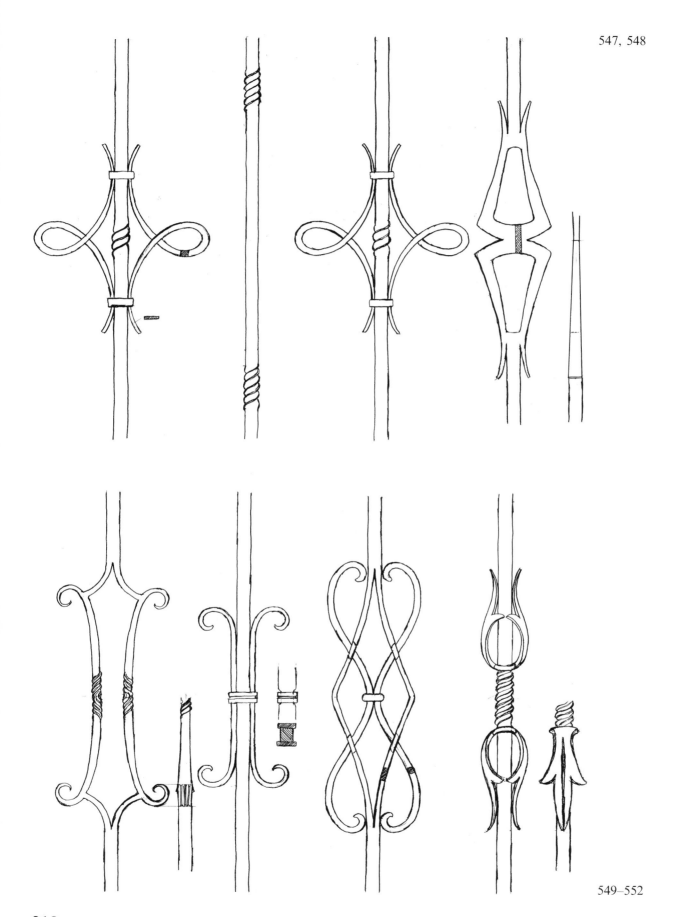

549–552

218

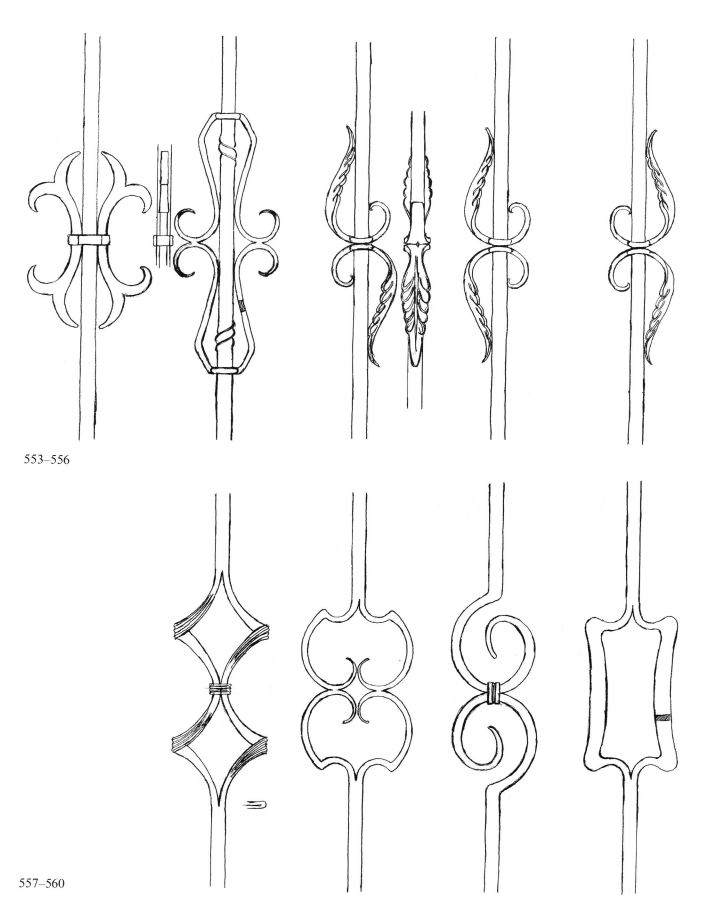

553–556

557–560

219

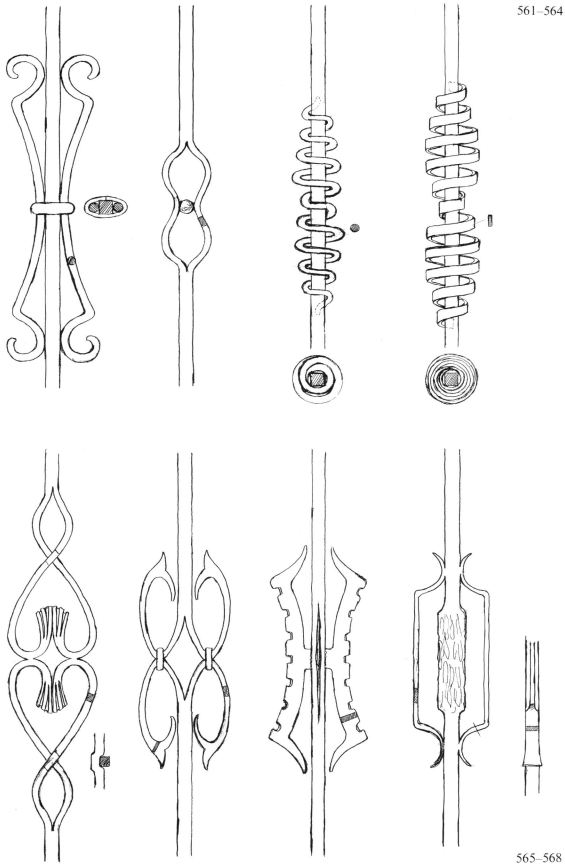

220

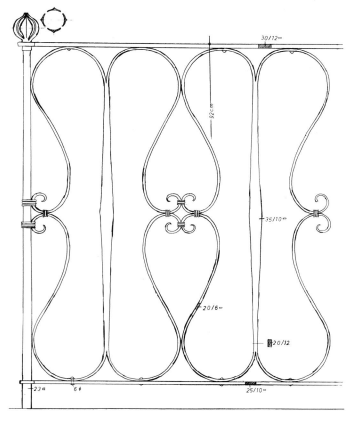

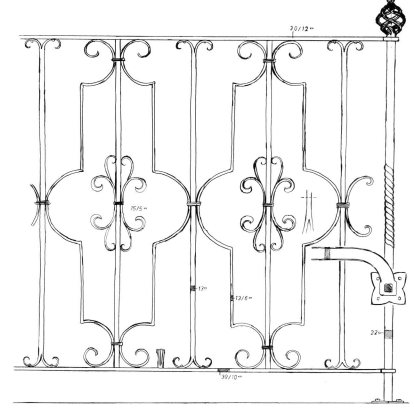

574

575

576

577

588

589

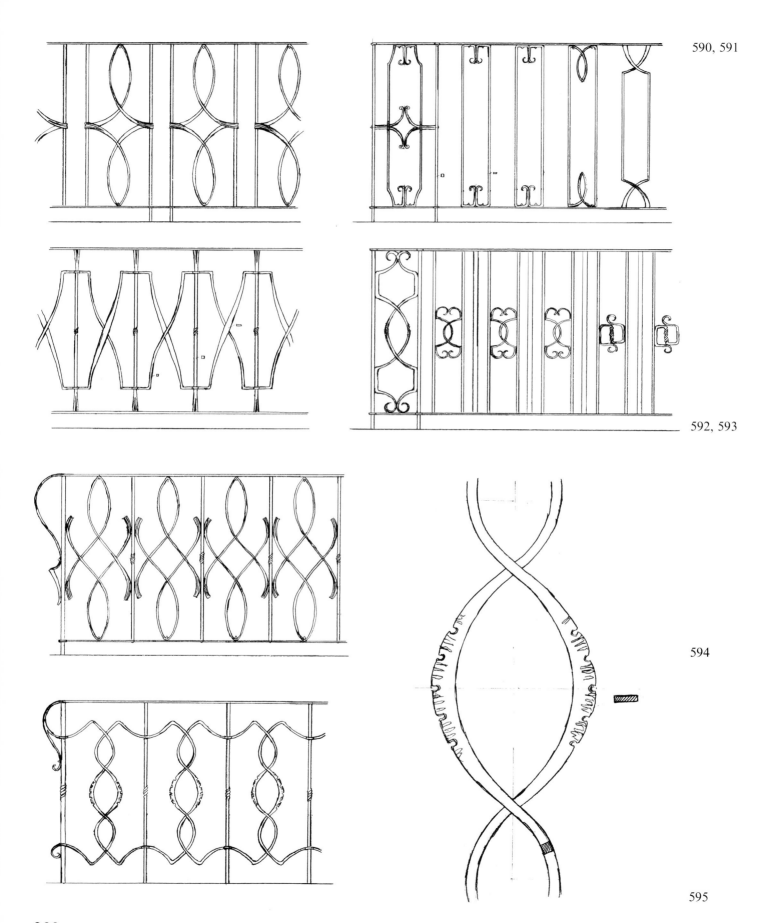

590, 591

592, 593

594

595

230

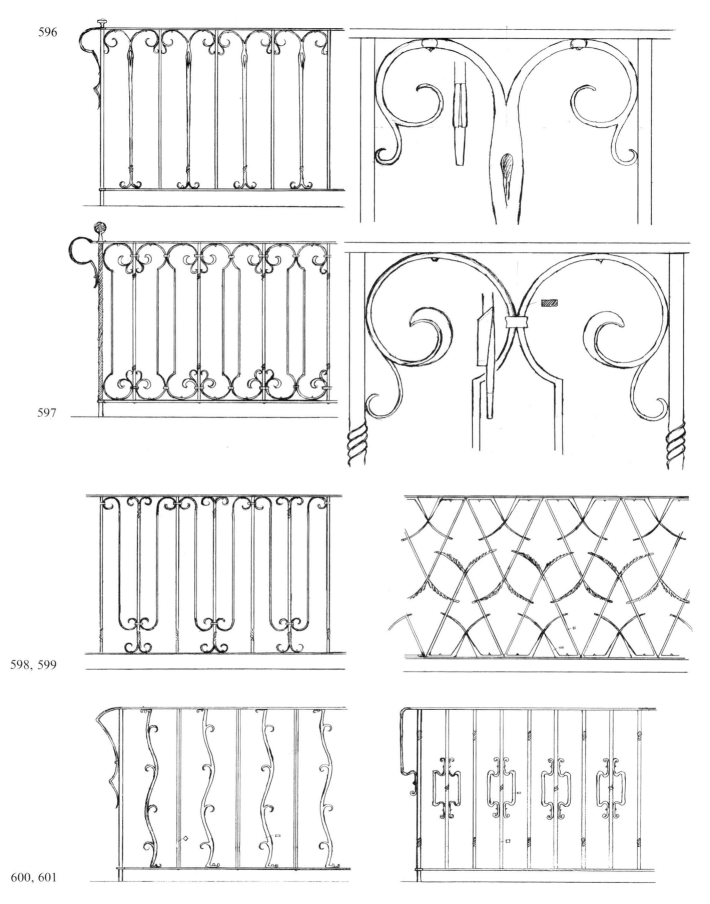

596

597

598, 599

600, 601

231

603

604

605

617

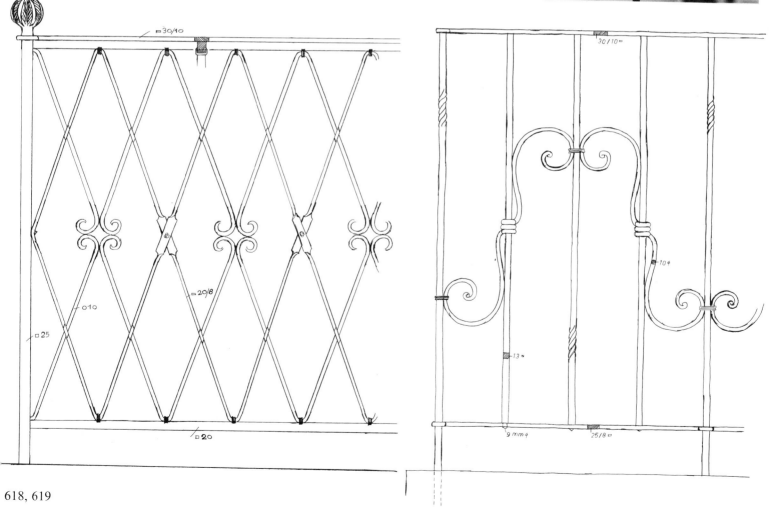

618, 619

620
86 × 125 cm

▱ 30/12

▱ 25

□ 14

□ 10

▱ 30/10

621

Gartenmöbel

Garten- und Terrassenmöbel sind heutzutage meistens Industrieerzeugnisse. Doch finden sich immer noch Auftraggeber, die dem Kunstschmied ihre Wünsche anvertrauen und etwas Besonderes haben möchten. Sie lassen sich ihre Gartenmöbel „maßschmieden". Alle hier abgebildeten Möbel sind aus Quadrat- und Rundeisen-Massivstäben gefertigt. Das bewirkt den zierlichen Eindruck, obwohl sie gewichtsmäßig gar nicht so leicht sind. Sitz- und Rückenpolster müssen abnehmbar sein. Tischplatten werden aus verschiedenen Materialien gearbeitet, zum Beispiel aus perforiertem Blech, beiderseits mit Kunststoff verleimten Holzplatten, eventuell starkem Plexiglas usw. Hier möchte ich ein Wort zum Oberflächenschutz einfügen: Am besten hat sich für Geschmiedetes am Haus das Feuerverzinken und der Anstrich mit halbmatter Farbe bewährt. An zweiter Stelle würde ich dann Rostschutzanstrich als Grundierung empfehlen, darüber einen beliebigen Deckanstrich. Patinierung, Goldauflagen zur Verschönerung gewisser markanter Punkte der Werkstücke, dürfen nicht die handwerkliche Bearbeitung des ursprünglichen Materials, nämlich des Eisens, überdecken und verwischen. Für Gartenmöbel hat sich übrigens ein Plastiküberzug sehr gut bewährt.

Garden furniture

Nowadays most garden and patio furniture is an industrial product. But there are still clients who entrust their wishes to a wrought-iron craftsman, and want to have something special. They let their garden furniture be 'forged to measure'. All the furniture illustrated here was made of solid square and round rails. This gives the delicate effect, although in actual weight the furniture is not very light at all. Seat and back cushions should be detachable. Table tops can be fashioned from various materials, including perforated sheet metal, wood laminated with plastic on both sides, possibly thick 'Plexiglas', etc. I would like to say a word about surface protection here: for wrought ironwork on houses, hot-dip galvanizing followed by a coat of a semi-matt paint has proven effective. As a second possibility I would recommend priming with an anti-rust preparation and painting over that a final coat of one's own choice. Either a patina or a gold-plate embellishment of special prominent parts of the ironwork should not efface the handcrafted forging of the original material – namely iron. For garden furniture, moreover, a coating of plastic has proved its worth.

Meubles de jardins

Les meubles de jardin et de terrasse sont aujourd'hui presque toujours des objets de production industrielle. Pourtant, certaines personnes, désirant quelque chose de spécial, préfèrent confier ce travail au ferronnier d'art. Tous les meubles reproduits ici sont faits de barres de fer massif, rondes ou carrées. Cela leur donne une allure fine, bien que leur poids ne soit pas si léger. Les différents coussins doivent pouvoir s'enlever. Les dessus de tables sont faits de différents matériaux, par exemple en tôle perforée, en bois recouvert des deux côtés de plastique ou encore en plexiglas épais, etc.. Ici encore, un mot à propos de la protection: ce qui convient le mieux pour le fer forgé dans la maison, c'est la galvanisation à chaud et une peinture demi-mate. Ensuite, je recommande une couche de peinture anti-rouille recouverte d'une autre peinture laissée au choix du client. La patine et les applications d'or servant à embellir certains endroits de l'ouvrage ne doivent pas masquer le façonnage artisanal du matériau d'origine, c'est-à-dire du fer. Pour les meubles de jardin, le recouvrement en plastique a fait ses preuves.

241

622

623

242

624

625

243

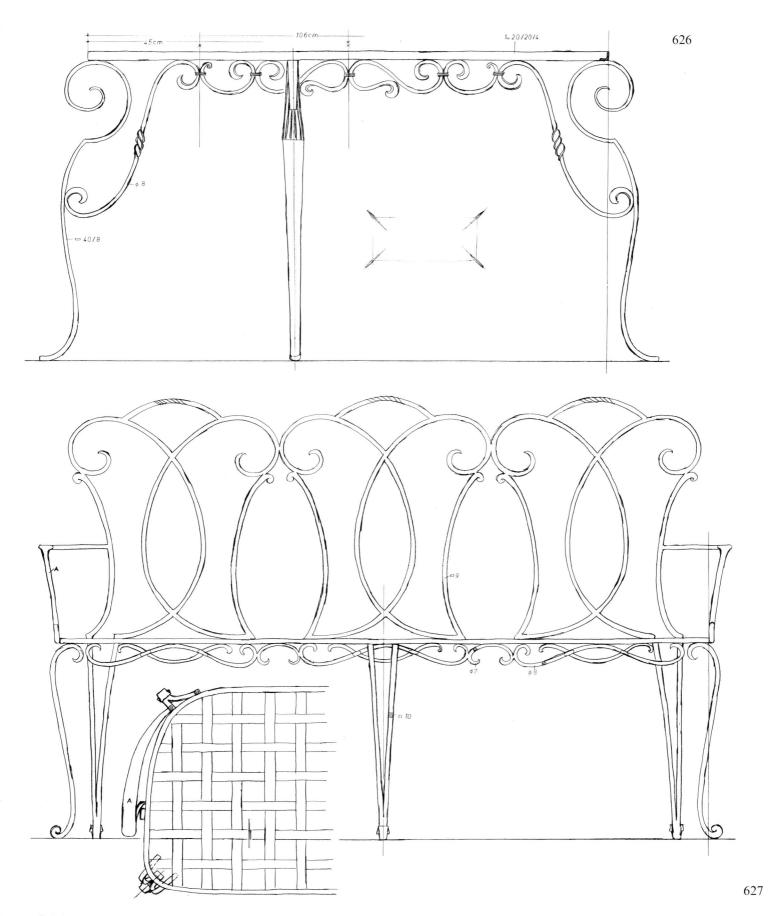

45cm

106cm

L 20/20/4

ø 8

40/8

ø 9

ø 7

ø 8

□ 10

628

Brunnen, Brunnenfiguren

Aus einem gepflegten Garten sind Brunnen und Brunnenfiguren in geschmiedeter Ausführung kaum wegzudenken, wenn man sie heute auch weniger aufwendig als in vergangenen Jahrhunderten zu erstellen gewohnt ist. Dem Kunstschmied sind hier mancherlei Möglichkeiten gegeben, dem Eisen oder dem Metall spielerische Formen zu verleihen. Wasserspeier und Figuren können aus Kupfer, Tombak oder schmiedbarer Bronze sein. In jedem Fall ist ihre Wirkung am Rand eines Wasserbeckens mit den optischen Spiegeleffekten unvergleichlich.
Abb. 629, ein vierteiliger Brunnen.
Abb. 630. Dieser Brunnen ist zweiteilig gezeichnet, kann auch drei- oder vierteilig ausgeführt werden.
Abb. 636a–c. Die geschmiedeten Teile sind für Transportzwecke leicht zerlegbar angefertigt: Oberteil, Steher und Rahmen mit Gitter.
Abb. 638. W = Wassersprengrohr mit Düsen.
Abb. 642. K = Kupferkugel, B = Blumenwanne aus Kupfer, vierteilig.
Abb. 647. S = Wassereinlauf in die obere und untere Kupferschale. Aus den Löchern im Boden der Schalen läuft das Wasser ab. W = Wasserrohr. Die Ausführung ist drei- oder vierteilig möglich.
Abb. 651. Der Flamingo ist eine elegant verkleidete Wasserbrause.
Abb. 657. K = Kupferblech, W = Wasserrohr, D = Detailzeichnung.

Fountains, Wells and Sculptural Fountain Figures

Wrought-iron fountains and fountain sculpture can hardly be excluded from the well-kept large garden, even if we are accustomed nowadays to choose a less extravagant style than was adopted in past centuries. The wrought-iron craftsman is given all sorts of possibilities here for fashioning the iron or other metal in ornamental forms. Gargoyles and figures can be of copper, tombac or malleable bronze. In each case the effect of the figures, bordering a pool of water and reflected in it, is incomparable.
Ill. 629. A four-part fountain.
Ill. 630. This fountain is pictured with two parts, but it can also be constructed with three or four.
Ill. 636a–c. The forged sections are made so that they can be easily stacked for transport: top, stand and frame with the railing.
Ill. 638. W = Water sprinkler with spray nozzles.
Ill. 642. K = Copper ball, B = flower tub of copper, four parts.
Ill. 647. S = Flow of water into the upper and lower copper bowls. The water escapes through holes in the bottom of the bowl. W = water pipe. The construction is possible with three or four parts.
Ill. 657. K = Copper sheet, W = water pipe, D = drawing of a detail.

Puits et ornements de puits

Les puits et ornements de puits en fer forgé font partie des jardins soignés, bien qu'actuellement on les fabrique avec moins d'ampleur qu'au cours des siècles précédents. Le ferronnier d'art a ici la possibilité de jouer avec les formes, de manier le métal à volonté. Les gargouilles et les personnages peuvent être en cuivre, en tombac ou en bronze malléable. Leur effet est remarquable au bord d'un bassin où ils se reflètent dans l'eau.
Fig. 629: un puits en quatre parties
Fig. 630: ce puits est dessiné en deux parties; il peut être exécuté en trois ou quatre parties.
Fig. 636a–c: les parties en fer forgé sont facilement démontables pour permettre leur transport (partie supérieure, partie centrale, cadre avec grille).
Fig. 638: conduite d'eau avec gicleur.
Fig. 642: boule de cuivre, baquet à fleurs en cuivre, en quatre parties.
Fig. 647: arrivée d'eau dans le bassin supérieur et inférieur. L'eau s'écoule grâce aux trous dont est pourvu le fond des bassins. W = conduite d'eau.
La fabrication peut se faire en trois ou quatre parties.
Fig. 651: le flamant cache un élégant jet d'eau.
Fig. 657: K = tôle cuivrée; W = conduite d'eau, D = dessin du détail.

629

▫20
▫30/20
▫30/8
▫24
M 1:1 1/4   ⊥ 30/10
25/10▫
40/8
▫20/8'
160 cm ⌀

630

B
18▫
20/8
100 cm ⌀
20▫
20▫
B

631

20▫
20/10▫
105 cm ⌀

632

147 cm ⌀

633

634

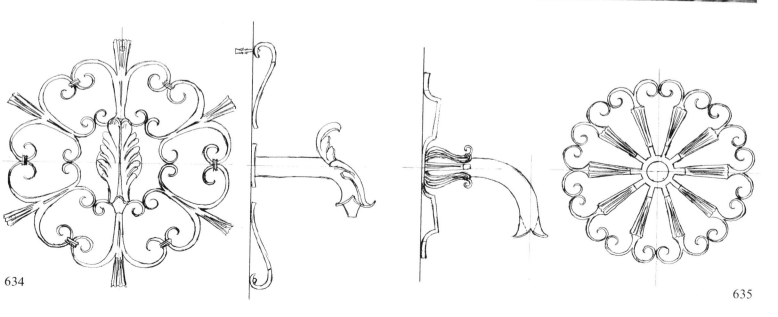

635

247

636 c   637

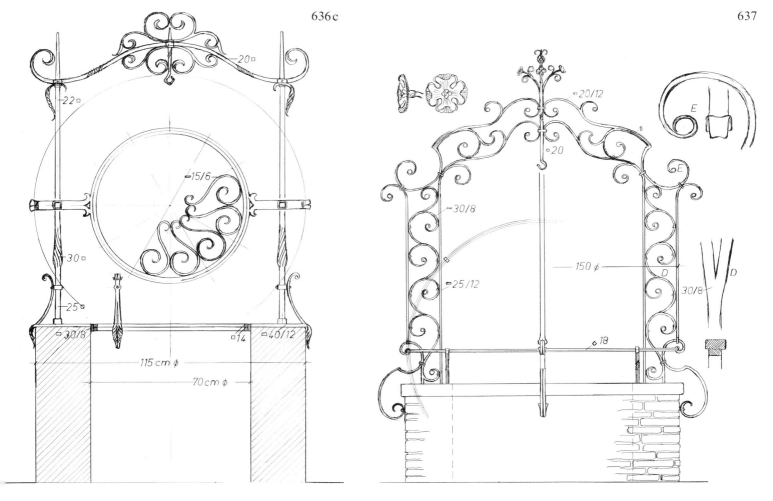

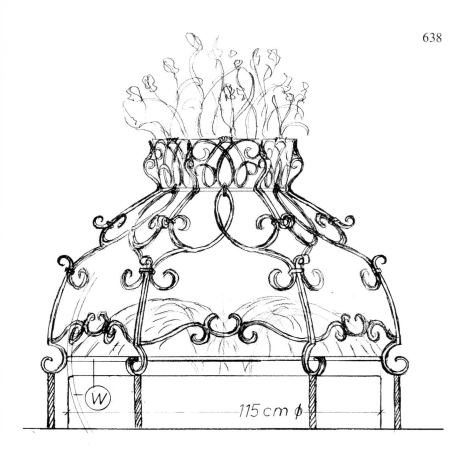

115 cm ⌀

W

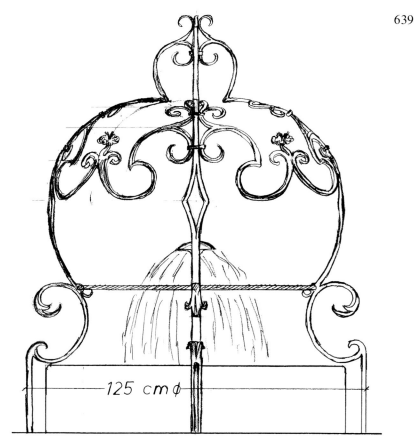

125 cm ⌀

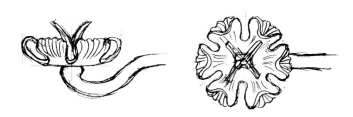

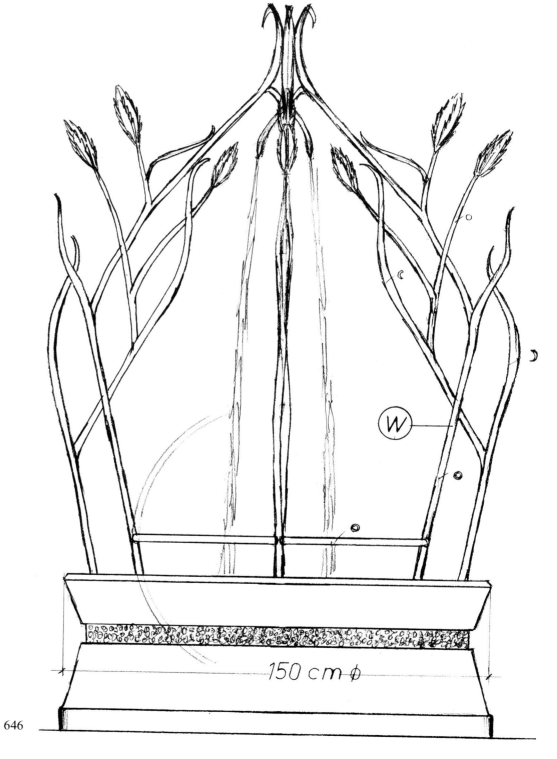

150 cm ⌀

646

255

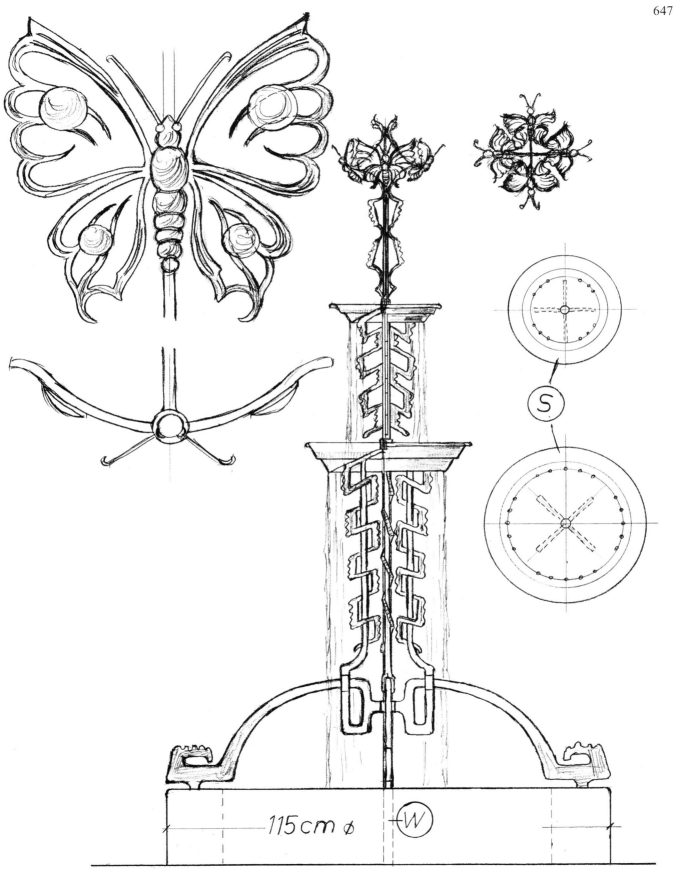

647

115 cm ⌀

256

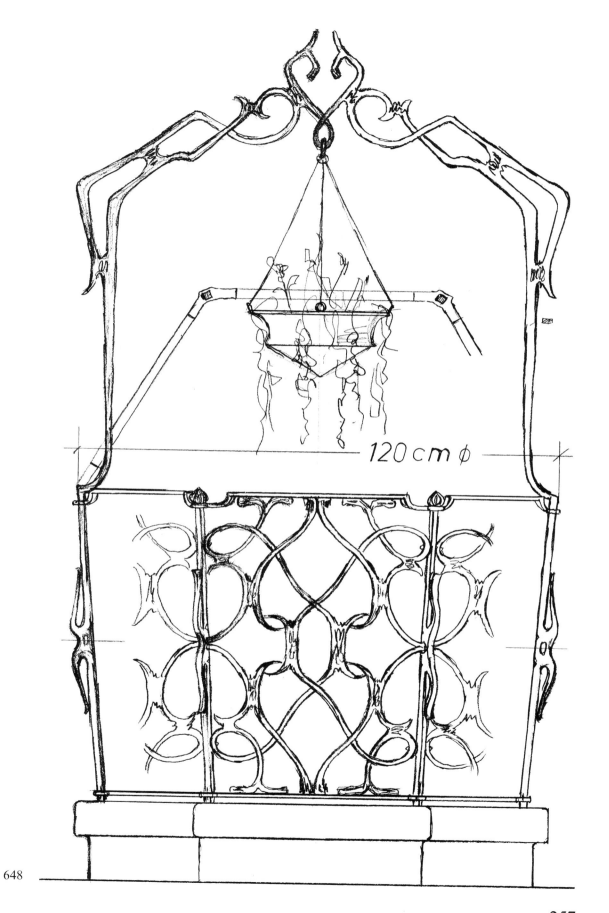

120 cm ø

648

1/24

1/12

120 cm ø

650

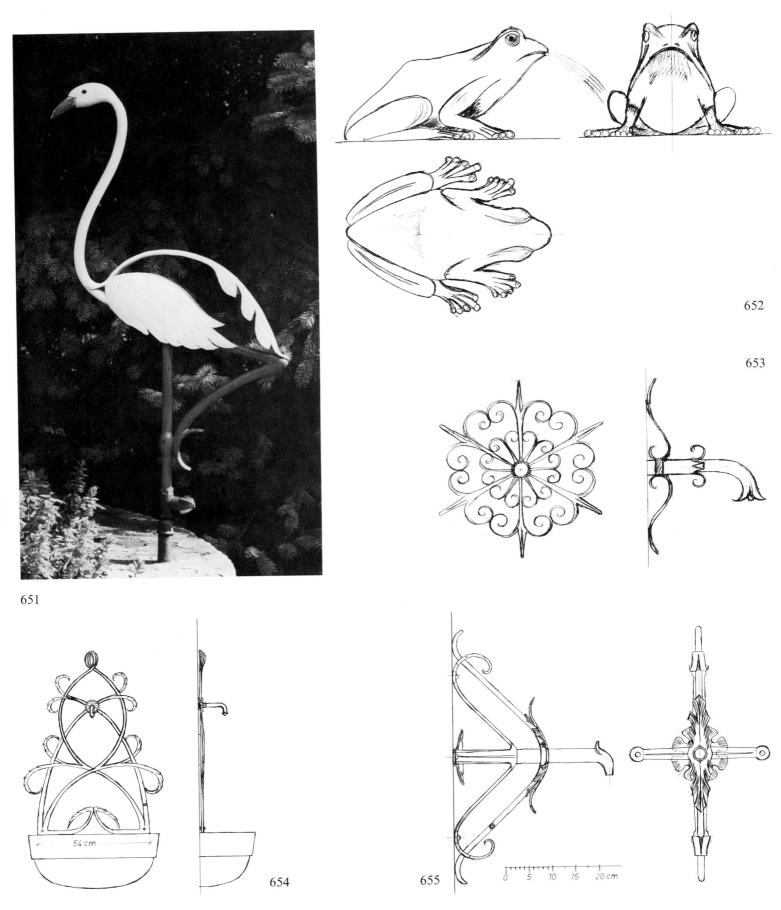

651

652

653

654

655

260

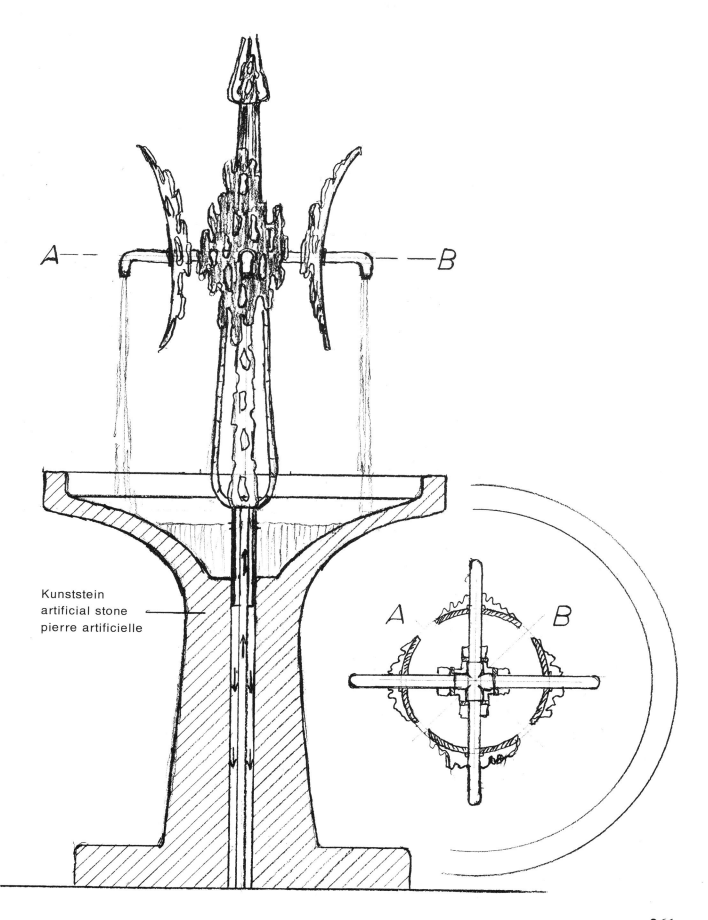

Kunststein
artificial stone
pierre artificielle

656

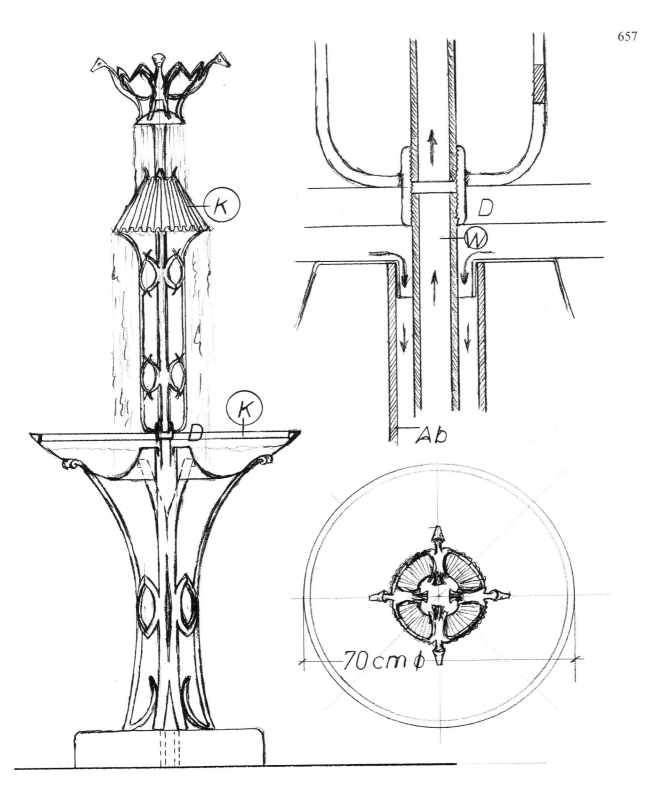

K

K

D

D

W

Ab

70 cm ⌀

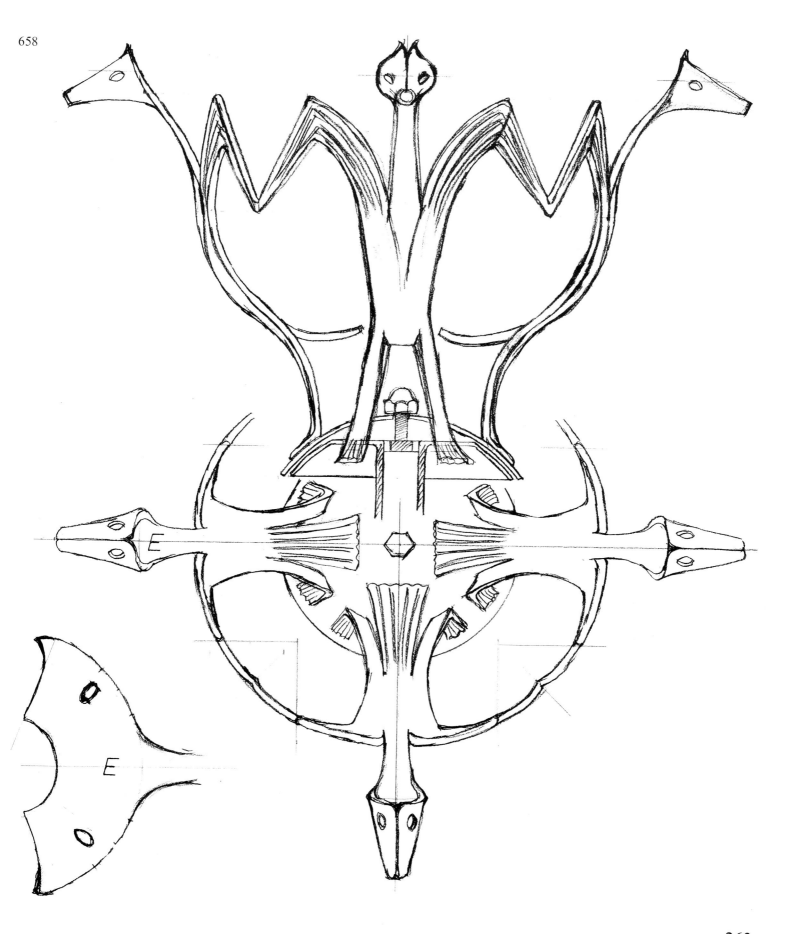

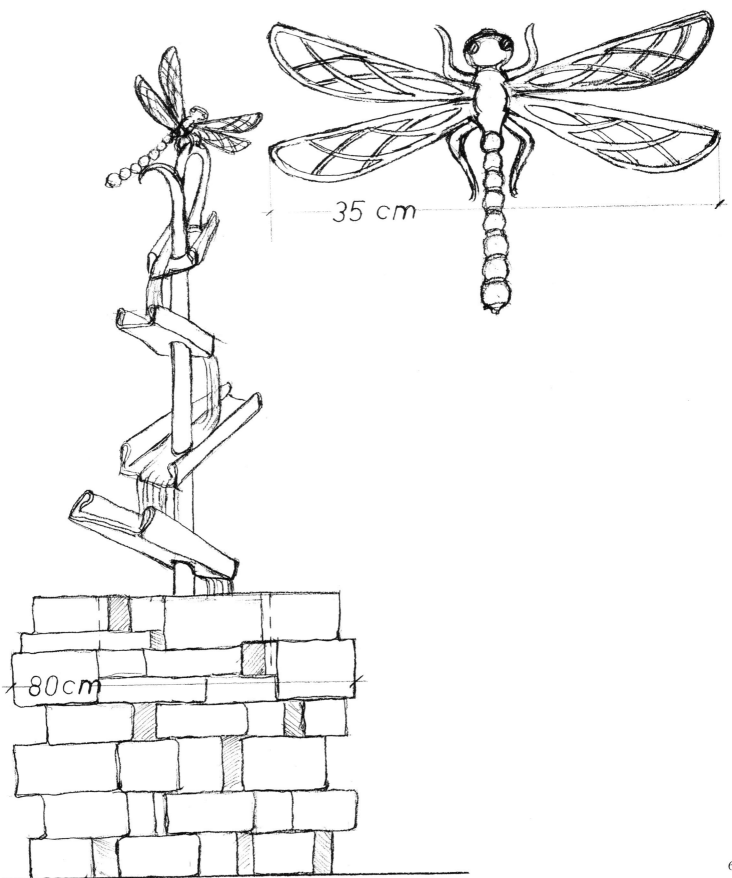

35 cm

80cm

660

Geschmiedeter Hausschmuck

Zu dieser Kategorie rechne ich individuelle kleinere Schmiedearbeiten am Haus, im Haus oder im Garten, die einen besonderen persönlichen Akzent setzen und als Blickfang dienen: Schwalben im Flug (Abb. 660), ein Vogelfutterhäuschen (Abb. 661), verschiedene Schriften und Ziffern (Abb. 677–698).
Abb. 662. Das aus Kupferblech wohlgeformte Kamindach schützt den Schornstein vor Witterungseinflüssen und ist gleichzeitig eine willkommene Dekoration.
Abb. 669–676. Die schmiedeeisernen Glocken haben einen wunderbaren nostalgischen Reiz, den jeder empfindet, der einmal den Glockenzug betätigt.
Abb. 663–668. Auch der eiserne Fußabstreifer zieht den Blick auf sich und ist gewiß der Wunsch jeden Hausbesitzers.

Wrought Decorations for the Home

In this category I have placed individual, small wrought ironwork pieces in the house, on the house or in the garden that give an especially personal accent and function as eye-catchers: swallows in flight (Ill. 660), a bird-feeder (Ill. 661), various letters and numbers (Ill. 677–98).
Ill. 662. The chimney covering formed of sheet copper protects the chimney from the weather and is at the same time a welcome decoration.
Ill. 669–76. Whoever has once pulled a bell-rope knows the wonderful nostalgic charm of wrought-iron bells.
Ill. 663–8. This iron scraper also attracts attention, and would surely be the desire of every house owner.

Ornements en fer forgé

Je classe dans cette catégorie des petits ouvrages individuels en fer forgé qui attirent le regard et donnent à la maison ou au jardin un aspect personnel: une envolée d'hirondelles (fig. 660) une petite volière (fig. 661), différentes inscriptions en lettres et en chiffres (fig. 677–698).
Fig. 662: le petit toit en tôle cuivrée protège la cheminée des intempéries et constitue en même temps une jolie décoration.
Fig. 669–676: les sonnettes en fer forgé ont un charme nostalgique que connaît chaque personne qui a déjà utilisé ce genre de sonnette.
Fig. 663–668: le décrottoir en fer forgé attire aussi le regard, ce que désire certainement le propriétaire de la maison.

661, 662

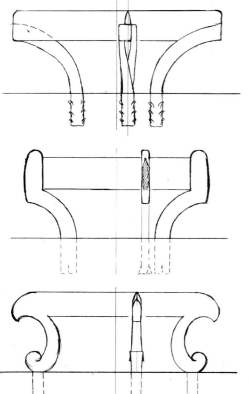

663, 664

665, 666

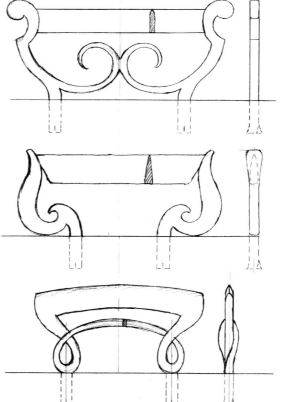

667, 668

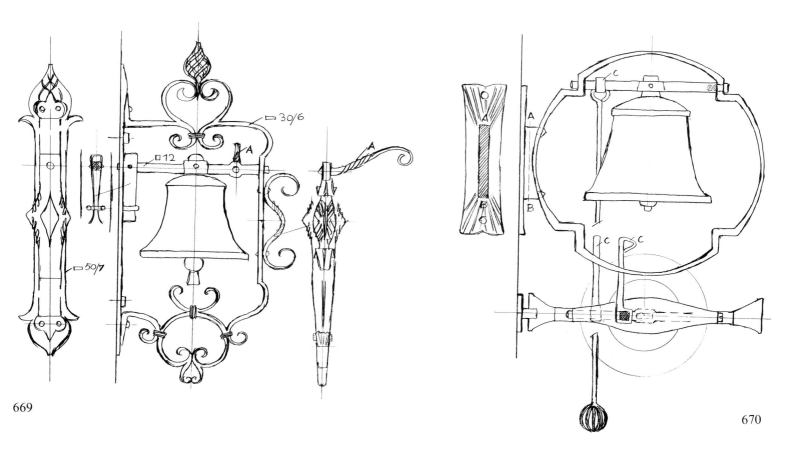

669

□ 30/6

□ 12

A

A

□ 50/7

670

671

□ 8

□ 10

□ 13

672   ⌀30 cm

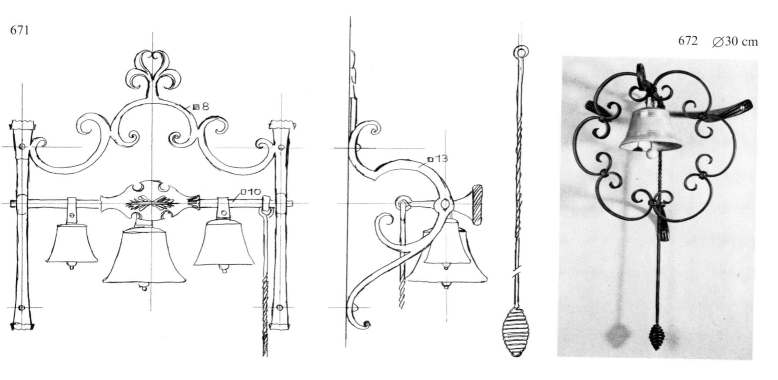

267

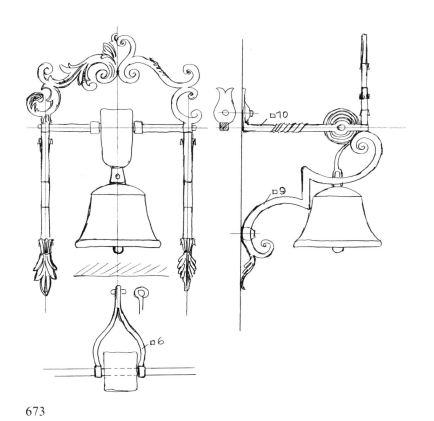

673

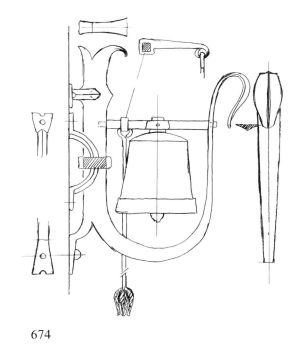

674

675

676

268

706

708

707

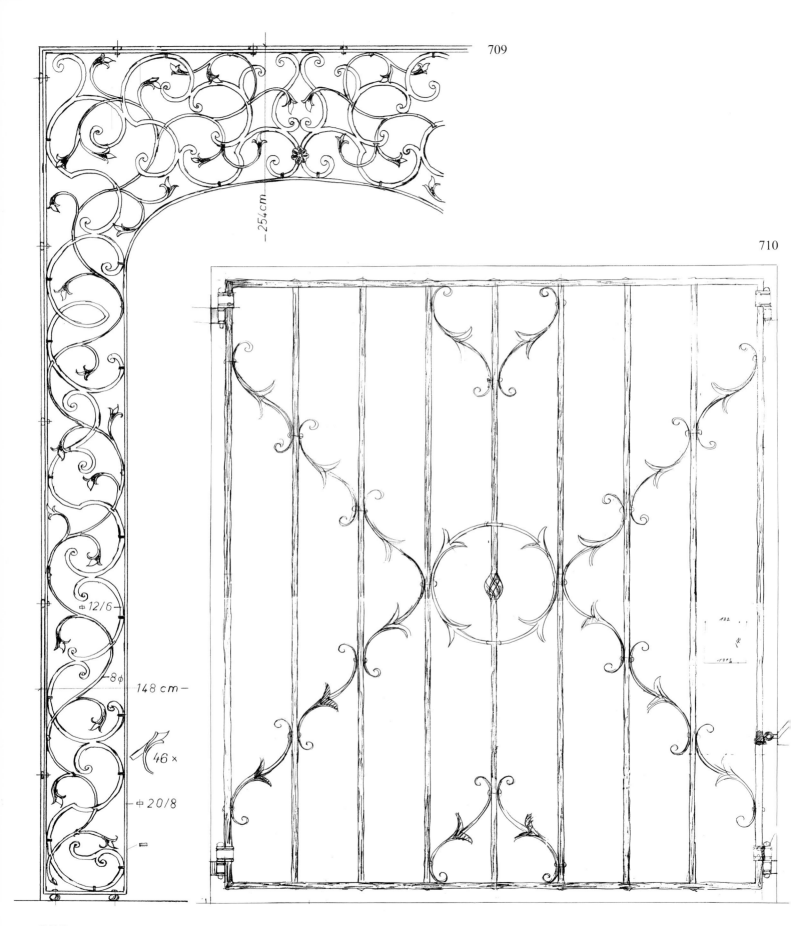

709

−254 cm−

710

Φ 12/6

−8 Φ

148 cm−

46 x

Φ 20/8

122

276

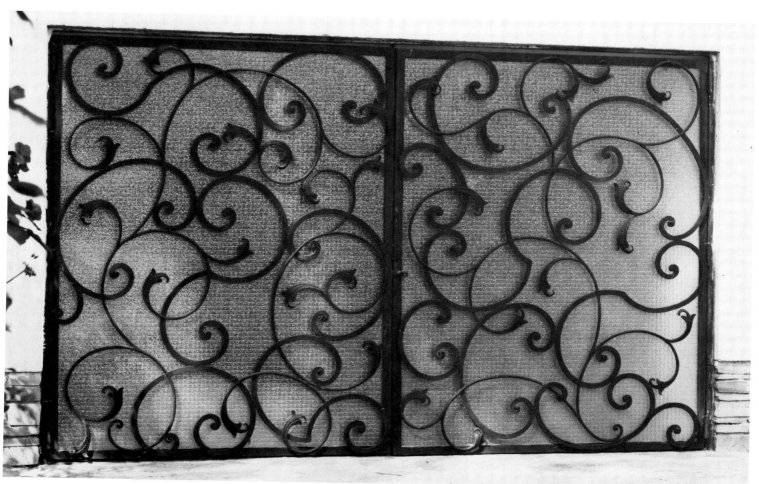

711

712

714

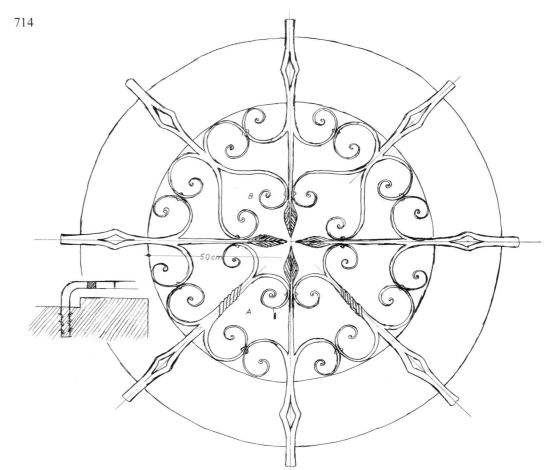

715

717

Die Burg Perchtoldsdorf

Als die Burg Perchtoldsdorf bei Wien dank eines Sanierungsunternehmens durch die Marktgemeinde wieder zu einem repräsentativen Zentrum von Ausstellungen, kulturellen und unterhaltenden Veranstaltungen großzügig renoviert wurde, erhielt meine Werkstatt den Auftrag die Kunstschmiedearbeiten auszuführen. Es galt die schlichten Formen zu finden, die sich dem Zeitstil des ehrwürdigen Bauwerks nahtlos einfügen. Nur so konnte der Auftrag zum Erfolg führen.

Abb. 720–723. Für das Geländer habe ich vier Musterstäbe angefertigt, ausgewählt wurde der Abb. 723 wiedergegebene.

Abb. 727 und 728. Turmstiegentüre mit gekreuzten Türkensäbeln.

Perchtoldsdorf Castle

When Perchtoldsdorf Castle, near Vienna, was generously renovated to become once more a representative centre for exhibitions, cultural activities and entertainment (thanks to a restoration project carried out by the community) my workshop received the commission to do the wrought ironwork. It was important to create simple forms which could form an integral part of the style of the old building. Only then could the work be successful.

Ill. 720–3. For the balustrade I prepared four sample balusters; Ill. 723 reproduces the final choice.

Ill. 727 and 728. Doors to the tower stairway, with crossed scimitars.

Le château Perchtoldsdorf

Lorsque le château Perchtoldsdorf près de Vienne a été généreusement rénové grâce à une entreprise de la commune qui en a fait un centre représentatif d'expositions et de réunions culturelles, j'ai reçu commande d'exécuter les travaux de ferronnerie d'art. Il fallait trouver les formes simples qui s'adaptaient au style de l'époque de ce bâtiment vénérable. C'est seulement de cette façon que le résultat a pu être satisfaisant et l'entreprise couronnée de succès.

Fig. 720–723: pour la balustrade, j'ai fabriqué 4 échantillons de barreaux. C'est celui de la fig. 723 qui a été retenu.

Fig. 727 et 728: porte de montée de tour avec cimeterres croisés.

718

Abb. 729 und 730. Turmaufgangsgeländer mit Türkenkopf. Die türkischen Attribute sollen an die Belagerungen Wiens von 1529 und 1683 erinnern.
Abb. 725, 726, 735. Lüster und Wandarme für die Beleuchtung des Rittersaals.
Abb. 734. Wegweiser zur Burg mit indirekter Beleuchtung.

Ill. 729 and 730. Tower stairway railing with a Turk's head. The Turkish elements are a reminder of the sieges of Vienna in 1529 and 1683.
Ill. 725, 726, 735. Chandeliers and brackets for lighting the knights' hall.
Ill. 734. Guide-post to the castle, with indirect lighting.

Fig. 729 et 730: rampe de montée de tour avec tête de Turc. Les attributs turcs doivent rappeler le siège de Vienne de 1529 et 1683.
Fig. 725, 726, 735: lustres et appliques pour l'éclairage de la salle des chevaliers.
Fig. 734: poteau indicateur du château avec élairage indirect.

719

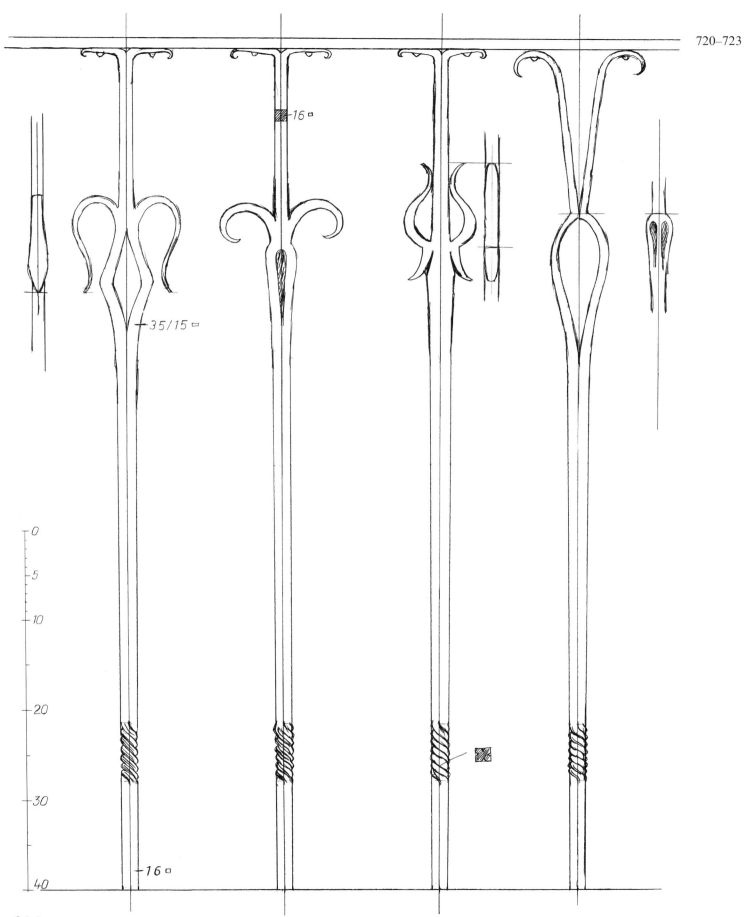

16 ◻

35/15 ◻

0

5

10

20

30

16 ◻

40

284

725

726

728

731

① Rohr
tube
732   tuyau

292

733

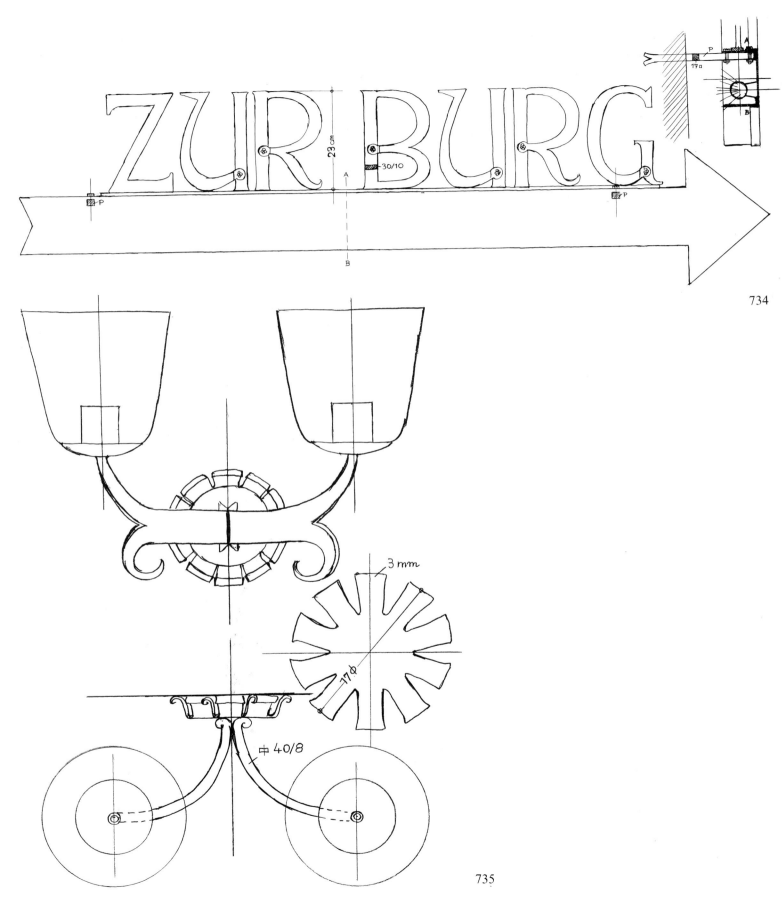

734

735

294